Career Development for Transitioning Veterans

Carmen Stein-McCormick

Debra S. Osborn

Seth C. W. Hayden

Dan Van Hoose

with

Military Consultants:

Thomas McCormick, USN (Ret.)

Major C. Camille LaDrew, USAF

National Career Development Association
A founding division of the American Counseling Association

Library of Congress Cataloging-in-Publication Data

Stein-McCormick, Carmen.
  Career development for transitioning veterans / Carmen Stein-McCormick,
Debra S. Osborn, Seth C. W. Hayden, Dan Van Hoose ; with military
consultants Tom McCormick, Major Camille LaDrew. -- First edition.
      pages cm

ISBN 978-1-885333-37-7

1. Veterans--Employment--United States. 2. Veterans--Vocational
guidance--United States. 3. Counseling--Handbooks, manuals, etc.
4. Veterans--United States--Psychology. 5. Veterans--United States--Social
conditions. 6. Career changes--United States
I. Title.
    UB357.S795 2012
  362.86'840973--dc23

                        2012047841

National Career Development Association
A founding division of the American Counseling Association

NCDA opposes discrimination against any individual based on age, culture, disability, ethnicity, race, religion/spirituality, creed, gender, gender identity and expression, sexual orientation, marital/partnership status, language preference, socioeconomic status, or any other personal characteristic not specifically relevant to job performance. (Approved by the NCDA Board – August 2011)

Printed in the United States of America

ABOUT THE AUTHORS

Carmen Stein-McCormick is a Licensed Mental Health Counselor in private practice specializing in working with service members and their families. She is also a consultant for DoD, working with service members and their families overseas and in the continental United States, as well as consulting for the Florida Guard and Reserves. Carmen served in the Army and used her GI Bill benefits to earn her bachelor's degree in Psychology from the University of Tampa, a master's degree in Counselor Education and a Ph.D. in Counselor Education and Supervision with an emphasis in Military Counseling from the University of South Florida.

Debra S. Osborn is an Assistant Professor in the Educational Psychology and Learning Systems Department at Florida State University. Prior to that, she spent 14 years at the University of South Florida as a counselor educator. Her research interests include the design and use of technology in counseling, innovation and effectiveness in counselor education, and the design and use of assessments in career services. She is an NCDA fellow (2010), past president of the NCDA (2012), and of the Florida Career Development Association (2004-2007).

Seth C. W. Hayden is the Program Director of Career Advising, Counseling, and Programming at the Florida State University Career Center. Seth has provided career and personal counseling in community agencies, secondary school, and university settings. He has focused on the issues of military personnel and their families both in his research and practice, and he has extensive experience providing career counseling to military personnel and veterans suffering from traumatic brain injuries. He has researched the collaboration between civilian and military service providers supporting families during deployment. Seth is the president-elect of the Association for Counselors and Educators in Government and continues to advocate for the needs of our military population and their families.

Dan Van Hoose enlisted in the Air Force after attending St. Petersburg Junior College for one year as a music major and served 21 years on active duty. He was a Munitions Specialist for six years, an Air Force Recruiter for 13 years, and a First Sergeant his final two years prior to retiring. Tours of duty were in Turkey, the United Kingdom, Lakeland, FL, St. Louis, MO, and Tyndall AFB, FL. After retiring from active duty, Dan attended the University of South Florida on the GI Bill and earned a Master of Arts degree in Counselor Education. He has been employed in the Career Center at the University of South Florida for 24 years and holds the position of Assistant Director.

ABOUT THE MILITARY CONSULTANTS

Tom McCormick retired from the Navy after 32 years of active service. He is a Licensed Mental Health Counselor in private practice and has consulted with DoD, specializing in counseling military service members and their families. He is an Adjunct Professor in the University of South Florida, College of Education. Tom used his GI Bill benefits to earn his bachelor's degree in Sociology from the State University of New York and master's degree in Education from Providence College. Tom is presently a regional supervisor for counselors that consult with the military and their families nationwide and overseas.

Camille LaDrew is a Major in the Texas Air National Guard and works as a Deployment and Distribution Flight Commander in the 136th Logistics Readiness Squadron, 136th Mission Support Group, 136th Airlift Wing. She has more than nine years of experience working with the Air Force and is often called to offer life counseling to service members. Camille has a bachelor's degree in Interdisciplinary Social Sciences with an emphasis in Psychology and Criminology from the University of South Florida. She presented at Argosy University's Annual Symposiums on Responding to Trauma, Crisis, and Tragedy.

PREFACE

According to the National Center for Veterans Analysis and Statistics, the veteran population (ages 17 and older) will decrease from 22.7 million in 2010 to about 14 million by 2035. Many of these veterans joined the military right out of high school and thus have never had to engage in a job search. Often times, their careers were born as a result of Armed Services Vocational Aptitude Battery (ASVAB) scores and the needs of their military branches and their careers grew as a result of performance and training. In other words, they may not have actively engaged in the career decision-making process, and thus find it difficult to know where to begin once they have separated from military service. Veterans also have many resources available to them of which they may be unaware.

Many veterans choose to return to colleges and universities upon separation, but may seek the help of a career counselor or specialist in choosing their civilian career and related major. Career practitioners who have never served in the military or received specialized training on the needs of veterans as well as the specialized resources that are available for veterans will be at a disadvantage when trying to serve them well. Our aim in writing this monograph is to provide career service providers with practical information through the use of case studies, presentation of research findings, and sharing of resources that can in turn benefit the veterans that they serve.

The purpose of this book is to increase career practitioners' awareness of the transition issues and resources specific to veterans and to provide several examples of how a practitioner might walk a veteran through the career planning process. Case studies based on interviews with real veterans by the authors and military consultants are used throughout the chapters to demonstrate the thoughts and feelings involved, as well as career practitioner strategies for helping the individual make a career decision.

We provide a general overview of veterans in Chapter 1 in the hopes of providing a context of who makes up this population, and also to identify challenges. In Chapter 2, we apply the idea of career adaptability and Schlossberg's transition model to transitioning veterans, and in Chapter 3 we describe a theoretical approach to working with veterans and demonstrate the use of specific tools and resources in the career counseling process. Chapter 4 provides a description of how career practitioners can navigate the career decision-making process with veterans experiencing physical, mental, and emotional injuries that may impact their career decisions. In order to demonstrate career practitioner strategies with a variety of transitioning veterans, Chapter 5 contains several case studies and accompanying practitioner interventions. Finally, with the influx of veterans returning to colleges and universities, some career practitioners have been called upon to create and deliver a career planning class uniquely tailored for transitioning veterans. Chapter 6 provides a detailed account of the development, delivery, and evaluation for such a class. Several appendices are provided, including a glossary, a pre-separation checklist, a list of relevant websites, and a sample syllabus for teaching an undergraduate career course for veterans.

While the writing of this book was a collaborative effort, with authors contributing their thoughts to each chapter, primary authorship was assigned for each chapter. McCormick was the coordinator of the project, primary author for Chapter 5, and provided extensive case studies for Chapters 1–4. Osborn was the primary author for Chapters 1, 2, and 3. Hayden was the primary author for Chapter 4, and Van Hoose was the primary author for Chapter 6. The authors wish to express their gratitude to Tom McCormick and Major Camille LaDrew for their valuable input (specifically on mental health issues) and for validating the reality of the case studies presented. The authors also wish to thank Deneen Pennington and Mary Ann Powell at NCDA Headquarters for supporting this project, and Bob Miles and the NCDA Veterans Task Force. A special thank you goes to Robert Reardon, Professor Emeritus at Florida State University and past chair of the NCDA Publications Development Council throughout all the stages of this project, who, along with the reviewers of the Publications Development Council, provided extensive feedback on the manuscript. A final thank you goes to the servicewomen and servicemen who have sacrificed so much for our country through their service in the Armed Services. We dedicate this book to them, and we hope that it will equip career counselors and specialists with resources and approaches to serving the veterans that seek their help with career decisions.

vi

TABLE OF CONTENTS

Chapter 1. Understanding Today's Veterans and Their Needs

Veterans seeking career services often present unique needs as well as strengths due to their experiences in the Armed Services. Consider the following:

- A young private loses her arm the first week she is sent to Iraq.

- A Guard member returns home to find his civilian job has been eliminated and his car has been repossessed.

- A Sergeant Major returns home after his 5th deployment and is beginning to show signs of PTSD.

These examples are from real military men and women who were facing the transition from military to civilian life. Their concerns are not compartmentalized into boxes of career, family, finances, and the like, but are blended and compressed. While these complexities are true for many of our clients, the experiences of a veteran is unique, and in order to be effective, a career practitioner needs to be knowledgeable of not only the unique issues and barriers veterans face as they transition from military into civilian life, but also of strategies and resources available to optimize the likelihood of a successful transition. For example, for many military members, life is filtered through the needs of the service branch. Therefore, upon separation from service, one's life needs to be decompressed, unwrapped, and re-organized without the military service framework serving as the definer for the individual and his or her family. While the time required for a successful military-to-civilian life transition to occur is unique to each veteran, most veterans do not have the luxury of taking a year or two to re-integrate before engaging back into the world of civilian work. This can add to the challenge of a career practitioner working with this population.

Today's Veteran

"Veterans" are defined as individuals who have "served in the active duty military, Coast Guard, uniformed Public Health Service, and the uniformed National Oceanic and Atmospheric Administration, reservists called to active duty, and those disabled while on active duty training" (U.S Department of Veterans Affairs (VA), 2010, p. 51). Not included are those who are currently serving in the military, those for whom active duty only included training, those who were dishonorably discharged, and those who were "separated" but returned to active duty. The term "separation" refers to the process of separating from active duty.

Demographics

According to the National Center for Veterans Analysis and Statistics (2010), the projected veteran population for 2012 is 22,234,000, with 8.3% female veterans. The majority of the military are 83% Caucasian, with nearly 9% Black, 5% Hispanic, and 3% other. While the overall population of veterans is projected to decrease by 2036 to about 14 million, female veterans are expected to nearly double by that time.

The 2010 National Survey of Veterans produced by the VA provides the following statistics: most veterans are

- 55 years or older (64%);

- non-Hispanic (95%);

- White (84%) as compared to Black/ African American (11%);

- male (92%);

- married (70%); and

- have no dependent children (69%).

As for educational level, many veterans have some college credit or associate's followed by those with a high school di less (31%), a bachelor's degree or high and a master's degree or higher (12%)

Women Warriors

Today's veterans are very dif ones encountered in the past. Un past wars where all but a few v now looking at a military force of 8% females. Women veterans or women warriors may have unique experiences that add to the complexity of the career counseling process. One such experience that is common for one out of five women warriors is the experience of military sexual trauma (MST; see Appendix A for definition), including any sexual activity against the veteran where she was not a willing participant. Red flags of MST include other diagnoses such as post-traumatic stress disorder (PTSD), anxiety disorders, depression or other mood disorders, and substance abuse.

In a recent study (Katz, Cojucar, Davenport, Pedram & Lindl, 2010) of 215 veterans (183 men, 32 women) from Operation Iraqi Freedom and Operation Enduring Freedom, 16.3% reported MST (of that 16%, 22 were men and 13 were women), and 15 of these reported enduring sexual harassment or unwanted sexual advances weekly or daily during their tour of duty. Those who had endured MST had the most symptoms and difficulties with general readjustment, intimate relationship problems, social difficulties, post-traumatic stress disorder (PTSD) symptoms, and career challenges. Specific career challenges included feeling pressured to work, unmotivated ˙ work, wanting to work but not being able to, ˙ˉg difficulty finding a job, and not knowing ˙ do next. According to Major Carmen ˉDrew, "Many women warriors may ˉv are in a position to reach out and ˉble services either due to her ˉtoms or purposely keeping ˉented in order to secure a ˉrance or join the Guard ˉnunication, August

(39%)
degree,
ploma or
er (18%),

ˉerent than the
of our
like many of our
ere males, we are

ves

ˉ pose
ˉom
ˉd has
ˉe states
ˉuipped to
where as the

second is to provide trained military groups that are ready to defend the United States and its interests all over the globe while often holding down their civilian careers. Often times called Citizen Guardsmen/Soldiers, today's National Guardsman are direct descendants of the militias of the thirteen original English colonies. Therefore, it is considered the oldest component of the United States Armed Forces. Since 1636, the National Guard has participated in every U.S. conflict from the Pequot War of 1637 to our current deployments in support of Operation Enduring Freedom (Afghanistan) and Operation Iraqi Freedom (Iraq) as well as local and national disasters.

Technicians or ARTs (Air Reserve Technicians for the Reserves) are federal civil service employees of their units for whom participating in the unit as a traditional Guardsman or Reservist is a condition of employment. During the week, technicians work in the same job they fill on drill weekends. Individual Mobilization Augmentees (IMA)/Traditional is what most people would call a "weekend warrior" job in which "citizen soldiers" work a regular civilian job but train with their unit once a month. If activated and mobilized, they are required to drop everything and report to active duty. After completion of 20 years of satisfactory service, a Guard member is eligible to retire, but they will not receive payments until age 60. Even the term "weekend warrior" has been used less during the recent conflicts in Iraq and Afghanistan. Many Guard members face additional challenges of transition from civilian to military back to civilian without many of the tangible supports those on full-time active duty receive.

Career Concerns Specific to Veterans

In addition to career concerns that most individuals face, such as career exploration, identifying career options, and job searching, veterans experience unique concerns as a result of their experiences. These include unemployment rates, wages, and differences in job responsibility.

This section reflects on these concerns as related to all branches of the military, women warriors, and the National Guard.

Unemployment Rates

According to the U.S. Department of Veterans Affairs (2008), unemployment rates for "Recently Separated Service members" (RSS) who are looking for work was reported at about 10%. That same report identified 45% as working, and the same amount are not working and also not looking for work. The Bureau of Labor Statistics (2012) reported a similar unemployment rate of veterans as 12.1% in 2011. The reason given for those not working included retirement (81%), disability (13%), stopped looking for work because they couldn't find work (less than 1%), being temporarily laid off from work (less than 1%), taking care of home/family (2%), going to school (2%), and other (1%). In a 2008 study (U.S. Department of Veterans Affairs) exploring the employment histories of RSS, the VA found that the unemployment rate for RSS was higher for veterans (4.4%) as compared to nonveterans (4.3%) and veterans who had been separated 6–8 years (2.5%).

More recently, the VA (U.S. Department of Veterans Affairs, 2010), found significant differences in hiring between RSS and a matched comparison group (MCG) of civilians. RSS are more likely to be hired by the government. In terms of employment, those in the MCG were more likely to be self-employed or hired by private companies. In looking more closely at hiring practices in the private sector, those RSS with higher rank or who had a college degree were less likely to work in the private sector, suggesting that "the private sector is not readily employing the RSS with management experience from the military or RSS with college education" (p. 23). RSS who lived in rural environments were 70% more likely to be self-employed, and those who were senior officers, noncommissioned officers, or disabled were less likely to be self-employed.

Wages

Earned wages were lower for RSS, especially for those with college degrees (U.S. Department of Veteran Affairs, 2008). The report mentions 2001 Survey of Income Program Participation and 2000 Census data as showing a significant difference in average incomes ($5,736 less, and $3,019 less, respectively) for RSS as compared to civilians. They report that 25% of RSS earn less than $21,840 a year. Unlike civilians, education was not significantly related to post-military salary. In this study, the researchers found that the strongest predictor for receiving a higher wage was having been a senior officer or a noncommissioned officer. They found that living in a rural or remote community and receiving GI Bill benefits were the strongest predictors for receiving a lower wage post-military. Education did not predict high wages to any degree. They summarized that predictors for higher wages for RSS included one positive predictor, i.e., rank (not including junior or warrant officers), and two negative predictors, i.e., living in a rural community and having used the GI Bill. The authors don't expand on the possible reasons for the negative impact of the GI Bill; however we explore this in the implications section of this chapter. Disability was slightly correlated with lower income, as well as having served in combat. Those RSS earning a lower wage tended to be enlisted personnel with less education than their counterparts. In summary, predictors of lower income for RSS included taking GI Bill benefits, lower rank, and less education.

Job Responsibility

The Employment Histories Report (U.S. Department of Veteran Affairs, 2008) showed that while education was not related to higher salary, it did predict the amount of responsibility RSS would have in their civilian jobs. Those RSS who earned a master's degree prior to separation were three times as likely to find a civilian job that required the same level or more responsibility. Those who earned a master's degree after separation were two times as likely to do the same, and having a bachelor's degree following military separation was also a predictor of having more responsibility. Rank and use of the GI

Bill were negative predictors of comparable responsibility in civilians jobs, that is, RSS who were senior officers were 70% less likely to have a civilian job with the same or more responsibility, and those who used the GI Bill benefits were also less likely to have a civilian job with the same or more responsibility. Possible reasons for the finding of the impact of the GI Bill were not given, but we explore this in the implications section of this chapter.

Unique Challenges of Today's Veterans

Today's veterans face challenges that differ from those in decades past. For example, the Huffington Post (Marchione, 2012) recently reported that out of the 1.6 million veterans from the Iraq and Afghanistan wars, 45% of them have filed claims for injuries related to their service, which is over twice the number that filed claims after the Gulf War in the early 1990s. The nature of disabilities has changed as well. Improvised bombs, improved body armor, and medical services have increased the likelihood that wounds that would have been fatal in the past are now survivable. More women veterans are filing claims of PTSD due to sexual trauma. In their study, Katz et al. (2010) found that those who had been injured either considerably or severely had significantly more readjustment difficulties on all the scales they measured: global readjustment, career challenges, health concerns, intimacy, social, concerns about Iraq, and PTSD.

Other mental health challenges include depression, anxiety, PTSD, substance abuse, schizophrenia, and suicidal ideation that may be associated with longer and more frequent deployments, and their conditions foretell a long-term national crisis. Researchers (Katz et al., 2010) reported that between 19% and 38% of recently returning veterans report having emotional difficulties. Another study reported that as many as 20% of Iraq and Afghanistan veterans and 27% of Vietnam veterans suffer from some form of invisible wounds of war such as PTSD or MST (Tanielian & Jaycox, 2008). Homelessness is also

a concern for today's veterans. According to the National Coalition for Homeless Veterans (n.d.), an estimated 67,000 veterans are homeless on any given day. To address the rise in mental health issues, the VA has developed a website and a *Guide for Mental Health Services for Veterans & Families* at http://www.mentalhealth.va.gov. Mental health services are available for veterans around the clock at VA medical centers via confidential chats at VeteransCrisisLine.net or text 838255 or crisis phone line (800-273-8255, press 1).

While education is a frequent option for veterans reintegrating into civilian life, there are concerns related to their knowledge of institutions who offer educational opportunities. Most veterans know about the GI or Montgomery Bills that can help fund their education, but they may not know the difference between these two bills (see Chapter 3), and more importantly, they may be overwhelmed with the number of advertisements from "schools" willing to use that money to provide training. They may be unaware that many of these programs are not accredited. Some occupations such as nursing and physical therapy require not only graduation from an accredited college, but also from an accredited program.

Counseling and the Military

While career and mental health counseling services have become more visible, there are still perceived barriers for many military accessing that help. Just because help exists, doesn't mean that every veteran knows about it. Even the term "counseling" has been used in a punitive way in the military. While in the military, fears of seeking counseling might include being seen as weak, lack of knowing exactly what the problem areas are, being stigmatized, feeling pressured to be "normal," or hurting their future career (Katz et al., 2010). These fears might carry over into seeking help as a veteran. Moreover, women may be reluctant to participate in counseling because of a need to "look tough." Veterans from different cultural backgrounds may present symptoms, describe their concerns, and cope in ways different from the majority population, which adds further complexities to counseling.

Career practitioners may also have attitudes toward the military that need to be examined. Stereotypes about veterans, personal attitudes toward the military or the "rightness" of being engaged in a given war or combat, or fear of not knowing how to help a veteran with their unique needs will likely negatively impact the counseling relationship with a veteran. According to ethical standards (Makela, 2009; NCDA, 2007), career professionals need to be aware of their personal values, avoid imposing them on their clients, and respect the client's dignity while promoting their welfare.

Implications for Career Counselors and Specialists

With this information as our background, we can identify specific implications for career counselors and specialists. First, a career practitioner needs to determine if a veteran's basic needs such as housing are being met. One might consider using Maslow's hierarchy of needs (Maslow, 1943) as a framework, and exploring whether the veteran's physiological and safety needs are being met first. Engaging in self-exploration or discussing educational options are unlikely to be useful if the veteran is having trouble finding food or shelter. Secondly, career practitioners need to be aware of the potential of concurrent mental health needs of veterans, and either ask specific questions about the veteran's mental health status or include them in an intake form. Katz et al. (2010) suggested that open-ended questions might not be the best approach; instead, ask specific questions about mental health concerns, such as "Have you had recurring nightmares since you've been back?" or "Have you had difficulty in finding work?" Questions such as these may help the veteran to think, "I must not be the only one with this experience" or "I didn't realize this was important, but come to think of it, I do have this issue" (p. 42).

Diversity issues such as age, gender, disability,

and culture may add to the complexity of the veteran's career decision. For example, if the average age of a veteran is 55, they are less likely to want to start over from scratch. They may not have dependent children, but may have concerns about college payment for adult children, coupled with paying for their own education. Career practitioners need to pay particular attention so as to understand the veteran's world view and view of self.

Given that the unemployment rates are higher for RSS, career practitioners can expect to see job searching as a major concern of many veterans seeking career services. In addition to general job search strategies, knowing about veteran-friendly employers, as well as specific tools to use with veterans (covered in Chapter 3) will be necessary. In addition, the findings that a college degree does not translate into higher wages for veterans may have implications for the job-interviewing process, where career practitioners can help veterans negotiate higher salaries through role-playing and rehearsing how to highlight their education and experience. A similar argument could be made for those veterans who were involved in combat. Given that so many military choose self-employment, career practitioners may need to brush up on their knowledge of community resources and grants (such as local small business associations) to support veterans in that goal.

The findings about the use of the GI Bill were troubling. It is unclear why those who take advantage of the GI Bill make less money than those who do not. It could be that some veterans are unfortunately applying their GI Bill to unaccredited programs that results in their needing to get additional training out of their own pocket. Another possibility would be that they are taking the money for financial purposes, or that they have not been acculturated to becoming serious students. While future research is needed to determine what else might be contributing to this finding, career practitioners can help veterans to identify, explore, and evaluate training options. Another possibility is that recently separated service members engaged with the process of moving out of the military culture into civilian culture can be overwhelmed when they add onto that transition the demands of adjusting to yet another culture (i.e., academic).

Finally, career practitioners might consider using technology to deliver career services. Some researchers (Wilson, Onorati, Mishkind, Reger, & Gahm, 2008) found that the majority of the 352 soldiers in their study were willing to use a number of technology-based approaches for mental health care (e.g., video teleconferencing, Internet-based treatments, virtual reality), and that 33% of those who were unwilling to talk with a counselor face-to-face were willing to try a technologically-assisted approach for mental health care.

Summary

This chapter provided basic demographic and statistical information on today's veterans, including information specific to women veterans and transitioning Guard and Reserves. Career concerns specific to veterans were described, including unemployment rates, wages, and job responsibility differences. Career counselors and specialists can play an important role in helping veterans transition to civilian life, combining the knowledge they already possess about helping individuals make career choices with information that is particularly useful to the veteran client.

References

Bureau of Labor Statistics (2012). Employment situation of veterans – 2011. Retrieved online http://www.bls.gov/news.release/vet.nr0.htm.

Katz, L. S., Cojucar, G., Davenport, C. T., Pedram, C., & Lindl, C. (2010). Post-deployment readjustment inventory: Reliability, validity, and gender differences. *Military Psychology, 22,* 41–56. http://dx.doi.org/10.1080/08995600903249222

Makela, J. P. (2009). *A case study approach to ethics in career development: Exploring shades of gray.* Broken Arrow, OK: National Career Development Association.

Marchione, M. (May 27, 2012). Iraq, *Afghanistan veterans filing for disability benefits at historic rate. Huffington Post.* Retrieved online http://www.huffingtonpost.com/2012/05/27/iraq-afghanistan-veterans-disability-benefits_n_1549436.html.

Maslow, A. (1943). A theory of human motivation. *Psychological Review, 50,* 370-396.

National Career Development Association (2007). *Code of ethics.* Retrieved from:ncda.org/aws/NCDA/pt/fli/4725/false

National Center for Veterans Analysis and Statistics (2010). *Veteran population projects: FY2000 to FY2036.* Retrieved from http://www.va.gov/vetdata/docs/Quick-Facts/population-slideshow.pdf

National Coalition for Homeless Veterans (n.d.). Retrieved from http://nchv.org/index.php/news/media/background_and_statistics/

Tanielian, T., & Jaycox, L. H. (2008). *Invisible wounds of war: Psychological and cognitive injuries, their consequences, and services to assist recovery.* Retrieved from http://www.rand.org/pubs/monographs/MG720/

U.S. Department of Veterans Affairs. (2008). *Employment histories report.* Final compilation report. Washington, DC. Retrieved from http://www.va.gov/VETDATA

U.S. Department of Veterans Affairs. (2010). *National survey of veterans, active duty service members, demobilized national guard and reserve members, family members, and surviving spouses* (Westat Final Report Deliverable 27). Washington, DC. Retrieved from http://www.va.gov/vetdata/docs/SurveysAndStudies/NVSSurveyFinalWeightedReport.pdf

Wilson, J. A. B., Onorati, K., Mishkind, M., Reger, M. A., & Gahm, G. A. (2008). Soldier attitudes and technology-based approaches to mental health care. *CyberPsychology & Behavior, 11,* 767–769.

Chapter 2. Counseling for Life/Career Transitions

Case Study

Frank joined the Navy when he was 17 before graduating high school. Frank had many nonprofessional jobs, such as swabbing decks, shining brass, and cleaning toilets. These jobs were noncareer designated as Frank did not have a General Education Diploma; GED or high school diploma. A few years later, a Commander took an interest in Frank's ability and encouraged him to get his GED. Frank always knew that he wanted to go to college and have some kind of professional degree. Even though Frank had not had the best role models growing up, he always had the feeling he could do better. He felt like the Navy was giving the opportunity to better himself. Four years passed, and Frank received his B.S. in sociology. At this point, the Navy began having Frank teach courses in addictions and sexual harassment, which led to an interest and ultimately a master's degree in counseling. He was able to do this because he attained quick rank, progressing from swabbing decks to being in charge of building torpedoes, and finally as an officer in charge of one of the Navy's top schools. Because he was not out to sea, he was able to go to a brick and mortar school for his education.

Frank's family life had grown as well; he was now married with two children. He retired after 32 years of active duty service in the Navy with great hesitation, as he was not sure what kind of job he would qualify for in the civilian world. Even though he had his master's degree in counseling, he had never used his degree nor was he licensed to practice. At the age of 49, Frank had great military experience but was not sure where he would fit in the civilian world as he had joined the military at 17 and had never held a civilian job. For two years following separation from the Navy, Frank attempted to apply for managerial positions (because that is what he was doing in the Navy; it is common for retiring officers to look for managerial/supervisory types of positions) as well as teaching positions in electronics (because he did not have a license to practice as a mental health counselor). However, he was informed by many of the interviewers that he was overqualified or that he would be seen as "military" by the rest of the civilians.

Case Study Reflection and Chapter Overview

Frank had a variety of experiences during his military career that laid a strong foundation for his next career move post-military. Even though he had training as a counselor, he did not have a license or experience as a counselor. As is typical of many officers, Frank leaned towards management positions because of the leadership and management experiences he had gained in the Navy. As he moved through different *Realistic* type jobs and then chose a *Social* field to study, his self-knowledge became more solidified. However, his lack of a license and current economic pressures impacted his ability to find work within the area of his training. At age 49, according to Super's model, Frank should have been at the maintenance stage of his career. Instead, Frank found himself back in the exploration stage. In addition to needing to explore potential career options, he also had the pressure of finding a job, as well as mounting relational concerns with his wife. Addressing all of these needs and determining how to do so became the challenge for the career practitioner.

In this chapter, we will review the idea of managing change, explore concepts of career adaptability and Schlossberg's 4-S transition model, identify possible transition concerns, present specific career counseling strategies, and discuss when a referral might be necessary and to whom the referral might be made. We will return to the case of Frank throughout the chapter.

Managing Change

Change can be difficult. Whether the transition is anticipated and desirable or unanticipated and undesirable, or some other combination, managing the process will have its challenges.

People who are anticipating transitions are likely to feel more in control and thus less anxious about the decision than those who ignored the signs of an impending change (Ebberwein, Krieshok, Ulven, & Prosser, 2004). Beginning in session one, we want to instill the idea that individuals are in control of the transition process. Some things might be or seem out of their control, but there are many ways clients can position themselves for a positive transition outcome.

Military individuals are trained to adapt in various situations, many of them unforeseen. The career practitioner can frame the client's main goal in this transition from military to civilian life as applying those adaptation skills to the world of work. Veteran research from the Pew Research Center (Morin, 2011) identified predictive factors for easy and difficult re-entry into civilian life. Predictors of having a harder re-entry included those military who had experienced a traumatic event, being seriously injured, post-9/11 vets, being married while serving (only in the post-9/11 combat vets), serving in combat, and knowing someone who was killed or injured. Predictors of an easier transition included being a college graduate, understanding the military missions, being an officer, and being a religious post-9/11 veteran (i.e., attending religious services at least once a week). This concept of career adaptability will be addressed in greater detail in the next section.

Career Adaptability

While on the surface, helping a veteran move from a military to civilian career may seem very straightforward (identify the transferable skills, plop those into O*NET or a job search database, and move into discussing job searching strategies), the process may involve greater complexities. The need to find a job might be pressing, but the first question a career practitioner or specialist should consider is "How ready is this individual to move into the decision-making process?"

Career adaptability has been defined as the "readiness to cope with changing work and working conditions" (Super & Knasel, 1981, p.

195), with four dimensions: self-exploration, exploring the environment, decision making, and career planning (Savickas, 1997). Readiness consists of capability and complexity (Sampson, Reardon, Peterson, & Lenz, 2004). Chapter 3 details how these two components interact, but in a nutshell, capability has to do with a person's ability to make a decision and complexity refers to the number or intensity of issues in that person's life impacting the decision. A person who is highly capable and has few complexities will likely be able to make a decision easier. Someone who has trouble making decisions and who also has several other impacting issues (such as financial and family pressures) may have more difficulty in working through the career decision-making process. To jump into a self-assessment or job-searching strategy without determining where the client is in terms of readiness would be a premature move that could negatively impact the process.

For example, consider Frank's situation. He has a great deal of varied work experience, but most currently has been in a management role of a top school, and he is wanting to find similar civilian employment. What if his career practitioner, after some initial conversation, went to www.mynextmove.org/vets and using the military-to-civilian search entered "manager." This would have provided a list of 20 civilian job titles, mostly with the word "manager," "supervisor," or "administrator" in the keyword box. Then, the counselor asks Frank, "What do you think of those options?" This is when it becomes very apparent that this isn't a simple matching process for Frank. "Well, yeah, ideally, I'd love to be in a management position, but I've been looking for two years for those types of positions, and no one will hire you right into a management position, and the entry level positions don't pay enough, plus they say I'm overqualified for them anyway. Why is this so difficult? Everyone told me how I should have no problem finding a job, but look — I've been searching for TWO YEARS now.... I'll take a job — any job! Maybe my wife's right. I haven't had an interview in over three months. Maybe it's just because I'm lazy— that's what she's been telling my kids, that's why she threw me out of the house. Doesn't she realize how hard it is to get rejected day after day?"

By jumping into problem-solving too quickly, the career practitioner missed some key information, and the session turned quickly to other concerns. Frank's negative view of himself, coupled with family issues, were skewing possible options, and the career practitioner was now in the position of backtracking. Further discussion revealed concerns about an aging parent whom Frank wanted to help, a family that had withdrawn their emotional support, and feelings of imposition on friends for temporary housing, all of which were adding pressure to the decision. In addition, Frank's feelings of desperation and frustration became heightened, and a series of two years' worth of failed interviews cemented a negative view of the future. While Frank said he was "ready" to find a job, the level of complexity going on in his life currently suggests that he will need some help navigating through the process. Gaining a thorough understanding of each of Frank's concerns and assessing how adaptable he may be to this change before starting on strategies might have prevented some of the emotional meltdown.

Planfulness

At the heart of adaptability is planfulness (Ebberwein et al., 2004; Herr, 1992; Savickas, 1997). Part of the career practitioner's goal with Frank after hearing the concerns would be to ease that discomfort by co-creating a plan that outlines the steps they will take as part of the career counseling process, a plan that would also address Frank's real and perceived barriers. The career practitioner will want to help Frank reframe the current situation, to the degree possible, in a more positive light, as an opportunity to explore new avenues as well as the paths not taken. Reframing and changing a negative attitude is not a one-time event, but may need to be revisited several times during the counseling process. Ebberwein et al. (2004) stated that adaptive

individuals "get off to a good start, think about and plan for their future, anticipate change and react when they see it coming, are cautious about stopgap employment, and know how to achieve realistic goals" (p. 304). Being adaptive involves planfulness but also a positive attitude and approach to the transition. Anyone in Frank's position would have a difficult time maintaining a positive attitude. Schlossberg's transition model, presented in the next section, will provide a structure for examining Frank's situation and focus on developing strengths within each area.

Schlossberg's 4-S Transition Model

In 1984, Schlossberg developed the "4-S Transition Model," which identified four major areas to consider when helping a client manage a transition:

Situation — trigger; timing; control; role change; previous experience with a similar transition; concurrent stress; and assessment.

Self — personal or demographic variables; psychological resources such as ego development; outlook (optimism and self-efficacy); commitment; and values.

Supports — internal and external; stable and most likely to change; and support needs such as positive self feelings, encouragement, information, referrals, door openers, and practical help (Goodman & Hoppin, 1990).

Strategies — direct action; information seeking; inhibition of action; and intra-psychic behavior.

A career practitioner working with a veteran in transition might use the model to frame questions about resources and deficits for each of the components to better understand what is involved in this individual's unique transition. The first step is to "take stock" of the resources and deficits within each of the four areas. In doing this, the client also begins the process of "taking charge" of the transition. This is an important change, as the person is moving from an external to an internal locus of control, which is a vitalcomponent of career adaptability. Also important is identifying where the person is in their transition. Are they "Moving Into" or anticipating the transition, "Moving Through" or in the middle of the transition, or "Moving On," i.e., has the transition already occurred (Schlossberg, Waters & Goodman, 1995)? Each of these has different tasks and emotions. When someone is moving into a transition, it is a new experience, and the individual must learn what the rules and expectations are, while someone in the moving through stage might feel like they are in survival mode. Someone in the moving out stage may experience feelings of grief, relief, or excitement. In the example of Frank, he has moved from military to civilian life, but is still moving (or hoping to move) into the transition from military to civilian work. He is also in a transition with his family.

In working through the model with Frank, the career practitioner made notes on the handout below.

Frank's Completed 4-S Model

SITUATION	SELF
• Retiring from Navy, mid career • Feeling out of control • Role change • Similar transitions – when he transitioned into military • Concurrent stress —family, financial • Assessment: an "11" out of "10" on how bad it is • Duration of career transition 2+ years	• Feeling overwhelmed, depressed, anxious • Low optimism, but some hope for the future • Clear sense of skills • Solid recommendations from previous employers • Strong education • Doesn't like dealing with ambiguity • Believes there are options, but unsure of what they are
SUPPORTS	**STRATEGIES**
• Strong faith in himself • Spirituality – here for a purpose • Family not supportive right now • Good friends • Support group at church • Retirement steady, but concerns about the future • Marriage outcome unsure • Temporary housing, but needing something more permanent • Need marriage counselor referral • Need job search strategies	• Mock interview, focusing on problem questions • Create a job search plan • Referral to marriage/family counselor • Join professional association, attend conference (develop network) • Volunteer • Pursue licensure • Find more permanent housing • Cope with stress: prayer, friends, journaling

Once the career practitioner and Frank completed the first three sections, they were able to identify specific strategies, which became the goals for future sessions.

The Counseling Sessions

Traditionally, the first counseling session is seen as an intake session, with the career practitioner gathering enough background information about the client so that the career problem is understood within the context of the person's life. Schlossberg's 4-S model provides a structure for exploring transition-related issues. Other concerns for a transitioning veteran might include:

academic	family adjustment	reverse culture shock (Westwood, Black & McLean, 2002)
adjustment difficulties	financial	role ambiguity/identity confusion
career	lack of control	social networks
disability	mental health	spiritual
discrimination	military sexual trauma	stop gap employment
education/training	post-traumatic stress	translating military experience to civilian terms (Clemons & Milsom, 2008)
family	potential gains and losses due to the transition	

A career practitioner could begin by asking about the transition in general and listen for stated concerns, or the career practitioner could proactively ask about these, or list these on an intake form for the client to select, rate the level of concern, or prioritize. In fact, some researchers (Katz, Cojucar, Davenport, Pedram, & Lindl, 2010) have suggested that veterans will be more likely to respond to specific questions as opposed to open-ended questions because, when they see or hear specific symptoms, it normalizes them in a way, and they realize they are not the only one experiencing them. Once an understanding of the individual's main transition concerns are known, career counseling can continue with self-exploration, occupational research, decision making, or job searching, revisiting the issue of transition as needed.

Other Counseling Strategies

Researchers and counselors have identified many strategies for helping individuals manage their career transitions, as described, next.

- *Exploration:* Blustein (1997) and Savickas (1997) emphasized exploration of self and career options. In addition to exploring interests, values and skills, ask for a description the roles the veteran played in the military as well as accomplishments.

- *Information:* Rosenthal and Pilot (1988) outlined several types of information to help with transitions, such as the nature of work, job outlook, earnings, and similar topics such as those addressed in sources like the *Occupational Outlook Handbook* and O*NET.

- *Mindfulness:* Jacobs and Blustein (2008) suggested mindfulness as a coping tool to reduce anxiety for helping with employment uncertainty. People can become so anxious about the future with all of its uncertainties that they become unable to act in the present. The client is taught to be aware of the present moment (by focusing on deep breathing) instead of racing ahead to thoughts of the future that lead to anxiety.

• *Resume Writing:* Requiring a forward-thinking mentality, resume writing can reframe military experiences/skills into civilian language. Clemons and Milsom (2008) suggested using a DD Form 214 as a source. Other military forms describing the veteran's various responsibilities can also be used. The career practitioner may need to encourage the client to write in terms of personal contributions versus the unit's successes.

• *Review Previous Transitions:* To gain a better understanding of the current career transition, it might also be useful for the career practitioner to discuss a previous transition through the lens of the model, such as the transition from civilian to military life. By doing this, it is likely that core values and issues will begin to emerge (Robitschek, 1997), and the client will hear repetitive themes in his or her answer that may apply and provide solutions to the current transition.

• *Three M's:* Pearlin and Schooler (1978) suggested exploring the three possible responses to the transition. These include modifying the situation (by job searching or getting training), changing the meaning of the problem (reframing), or managing the stress.

• *Visual Metaphors:* Barner (2011) described using a visual metaphor technique in which a client describes a visual metaphor (from an image) that represents what he or she is feeling, thinking, and experiencing that day, and then chooses another to describe the future. For example, Jane may choose a rollercoaster to represent how she currently feels in her situation — out of control and going way too fast for her image. But for her future image, she might choose a sports car in which she is the driver and where she can go the speed she desires and encounter adventures.

• *Visualization:* Have the client visualize the details of the next career.

Resources Career Practitioners and Specialists Typically Can Share

Career practitioners have many resources that are appropriate for transitioning veterans, including career assessments, career information, decision-making strategies or models, and job-search strategies. Many colleges also have undergraduate career courses or may even have a special section such as the class described in Chapter 6, or centers on campus such as a Veterans Success Center. A campus environment also has many potentially appropriate referral points, such as the counseling center, student life center, spiritual groups, organizations for mature students, and so forth. Those not on a college campus may need to identify community supports for mental health counseling, local veterans' affairs offices, marriage/family counseling, grief/loss counseling, PTSD treatment, and vocational rehabilitation. While many career practitioners are trained to provide mental health counseling, they should always work within their boundaries of competence and provide referrals or seek supervision when a client's needs exceeds those.

Transition Assistance Programs

Career practitioners should know that service members and their families are eligible to receive assistance with transitions throughout their lives. The military provides a separation counseling process called the Transition Assistance Program (TAP), developed in 1990, with the purpose of providing information on employment and training opportunities to those separating or retiring military and their spouses within 180 days of that time. TAP is actually a law that formed a partnership among the Departments of Defense, Veterans Affairs, Transportation, and the Veteran's Employment and Training Service, a division of the Department of Labor. TAP provides workshops on all aspects of career decision making and job search, as well as information on benefits available to veterans. The five major areas reviewed in TAP include Employment and Career Goals, Education and Training, Financial

Readiness, Health and Well Being, and Relocation and Housing Assistance. Specific to transition planning, TAP has identified seven areas: self-assessment, exploration, skills development, intern programs, job search, job selection, and executing the transition. There is also a TAP specific for military personnel who were released because of a disability, called DTAP. While TAP participation is not mandatory, a study by the VA (U.S. Department of Veterans Affairs, 2010) found that more than 12% of transitioning veterans attended a TAP workshop, and 56% of these said it was useful or very useful.

The TAP website (taonline.com/Tap Office) reported that in a national evaluation of the program, those who had participated in TAP found post-military positions three weeks earlier than those who had not participated. The TAPS website (taonline.com) also has a page called "transition information center," as well as opportunities to post resumes, search jobs, and learn about featured employers. One of the forms used in TAPs that may be of particular help to career practitioners is the Pre-Separation Counseling Checklist (See Appendix B). Even if a veteran has not taken advantage of TAP, this form provides a useful structure and language familiar to the veteran that the career practitioner can use as a starting platform for career-related discussions.

"Vet Reps" or veterans employment representatives are employment specialists funded through the Veterans' Employment and Training State Grants, which provide funding exclusively for servicing veterans, transitioning service members, and their spouses. There are also Vet Reps available for veterans with disabilities, called DVOPS (Disabled Veterans' Outreach Program Specialists). Vet Reps provide assistance with job searching and training for unemployed and underemployed veterans. Veterans can locate a local Vet Rep online at http://www.taonline.com/VetReps/SearchVetRep.asp. Also, the Department of Veterans Affairs provides another useful website for career practitioners and transitioning veterans called

the Vet Success site (vetsuccess.gov/vetsuccess_in_transition), which provides an interactive map of the United States to help quickly locate state resources for veterans where they can begin the transition process by locating a career practitioner.

Supports for Military Families

Military service puts significant pressure and stress on military couples and their families. Deployment and reintegration can leave a couple with issues that most nonmilitary couples rarely ever have to deal with. When children are also in the picture, their adjustment to a new school and home, coupled with grieving the life that was left behind adds to the potential complexities military families experience when the military member begins the separation process. Career practitioners should be aware that the military also offers support for veterans and their families through the Vet Centers, specifically through individual and couples counseling, military and family life consultants (MLFC), and Military OneSource.

Military and Family Life Consultants (MLFC)

Through the MFLC Program, licensed clinical providers assist service members and their families with issues they may face through the cycle of deployment, from leaving their loved ones and possibly living and working in harm's way to reintegrating with their community and family. The MFLC program provides support for a range of issues including relationships, crisis intervention, stress management, grief, occupational, and other individual and family issues. Psycho-educational presentations on reunion/reintegration, stress/coping, grief/loss, and deployment are provided to commands, family readiness groups, soldier readiness processing, and other requested locations.

MFLC support is also provided to the Child and Youth Program and specifically for the DoDEA/CYP summer enrichment program. Support for these issues empowers individuals during the problem-solving process, increases individual and family competency and confidence in handling the stressors of military life, and ensures that issues do not impair operational readiness. MFLCs address relationship issues, stress management, grief after loss, occupational and other individual and family issues, and provide crisis intervention when needed. Information about the Military and Family Life Consultant Program (MFLC) is located at www.mhngs.com.

Military OneSource

Military OneSource uses a nationwide network of practitioners that provide short-term, solution-focused sessions that deal with veterans' adjustment issues, work life topics, and emotional well-being issues. A veteran might use Military OneSource to improve relationships at home and at work, help with marital issues, cope with grief and loss issues (normal reactions that would benefit from short-term counseling), adjust to a change in situation (such as deployment/reintegration issues), and address other concerns that are not medically diagnosable. The face-to-face individual counseling benefit is limited to 12 sessions. It is not designed to address long-term issues such as child or spouse abuse, suicidal ideation, and mental health issues. People in need of long-term care are normally referred to a military treatment facility and/or TRICARE. These sessions are prepaid by the Department of Defense as a part of the Military OneSource contract, and there are no out-of-pocket expenses to the military member or their family. During a brief telephone assessment, the consultant will provide a career practitioner that best matches the veteran's needs. Normally, career practitioners are located within a 30-mile radius of the caller. Callers are provided with all necessary contact details and encouraged to connect with the local practitioner as soon as possible.

Case Study Closure

Frank worked with a career specialist at the local Vet Center. During the sessions, the career specialist helped Frank explore and build his network. Frank remembered a friend he had met in the Navy who was now a licensed counselor in private practice who had challenged him to consider working as a therapist. He called his friend, who had many local contacts in the community and, through her network, was able to secure Frank a job at a managed mental health company. During this time, he worked towards getting his license, and currently is working as a licensed counselor in private practice, as well as, consulting for the Department of Defense, specifically working with military service members and their families. Frank has become a very well known counselor in his field and strives to help other veterans in their quest to integrate into civilian life.

Summary

Veterans who are separating face many transitions, some of which are similar to the transitions that nonmilitary individuals face when moving from one job to another. However, because of their unique experiences, veterans as a group may face unique challenges when transitioning to civilian life. Career counselors and specialists can apply the 4-S model of transition when working with veterans to help the veterans understand and process through their transition. Career practitioners can also make use of resources available through the military, such as Military OneSource and the pre-separation checklist.

References

Barner, R. W. (2011). Applying visual metaphors to career transitions. *Journal of Career Development, 38*, 89–06. DOI: 10.1177/0894845309359287

Blustein, D. L. (1997). A context-rich perspective of career exploration across the life roles. *The Career Development Quarterly, 45*, 260–274.

Clemens, E. V., & Milsom, A. S. (2008). Enlisted service members' transition into the civilian world of work: A cognitive information processing approach. *The Career Development Quarterly, 56*, 246–256.

Ebberwein, C. A., Krieshok, T. S., Ulven, J. C., & Prosser, E. C. (2004). Voices in transition: Lessons on career adaptability. *The Career Development Quarterly, 52*, 292–308.

Herr, E. L. (1992). Counseling for personal flexibility in a global economy. *Educational and Vocational Guidance, 53*, 5–16.

Jacobs, S. J., & Blustein, D. L. (2008). Mindfulness as a coping mechanism for employment uncertainty. *The Career Development Quarterly, 57*, 174–180.

Katz, L. S., Cojucar, G., Davenport, C. T., Pedram, C., & Lindl, C. (2010). Post-deployment readjustment inventory: Reliability, validity, and gender differences. *Military Psychology, 22*, 4156. http://dx.doi.org/10.1080/08995600903249222

Morin, R. (2011). The difficult transition from military to civilian life. *Pew Social & Demographic Trends, Pew Research Center.* Retrieved August 30, 2012, http://www.pewsocialtrends.org/2011/12/08/the-difficult-transition-from-military-to-civilian-life/

Pearlin, L. I., & Schooler, C. (1978). The structure of coping. *Journal of Health and Social Behavior, 19*, 2–21.

Robitschek, C. (1997). Life/career renewal: An intervention for vocational and other life transitions. *Journal of Career Development, 24*, 133–146.

Rosenthal, N. H., & Pilot, M. (1988). Information needs for initial and ongoing work transition. *Journal of Career Development, 15*, 20-29. DOI: 10.1177/089484538801500103

Sampson, J.P., Jr., Reardon, R.C., Peterson, G.W., & Lenz, J. G. (2004). *Career counseling and services: A cognitive information processing approach.* Pacific Grove, CA: Brooks/Cole.

Savickas, M. L. (1997). Career adaptability: An integrative construct for Life-Span, Life-Space theory. *The Career Development Quarterly, 45*, 247-259.

Schlossberg, N.K. (1984). *Counseling adults in transitions.* New York: Springer Publishing Company.

Schlossberg, N. K., Waters, E., & Goodman, J. (1995). *Counseling adults in transition.* New York: Springer.

Super, D. E., & Knasel, E. G. (1981). Career development in adulthood: Some theoretical problems and a possible solution. *British Journal of Guidance and Counselling, 9*, 194–201.

U.S. Department of Veterans Affairs. (2010). *National survey of veterans, active duty service members, demobilized national guard and reserve members, family members, and surviving spouses* (Westat Final Report Deliverable 27). Washington, DC. Retrieved from http://www.va.gov/vetdata/docs/SurveysAndStudies/NVSSurveyFinalWeightedReport.pdf

Westwood, M. J., Black, T. G., & McLean, H. B. (2002). A re-entry program for peacekeeping soldiers: Promoting personal and career transition. *Canadian Journal of Counselling, 36*, 221–232.

Case Study

Monica was 18 when she joined the Army. She graduated from high school where she did very well academically, but her family could not afford to send her to college so she decided to join the Army to get the GI Bill. During her four years in the Army, on the basis of her Armed Services Vocational Aptitude Battery (ASVAB) scores, Monica worked as an engineer and in military intelligence. Early on in Monica's enlistment, she injured her shoulders, but she was able to receive treatment in order to be functional. Monica progressed very quickly and received numerous commendations. Her plan was to make the military a career while attending college. Her plan quickly changed when her marriage became a "burden" to her career. Her husband, who was also in Army, was not as successful as Monica. After five years of trying to make things work, she made the decision to get out of the Army in order to get her degree and then return as an officer. Within two months after leaving the military, Monica divorced her husband. She really wanted to be a doctor, but felt she did not have the background training or support from her ex-husband to study pre-med. Her current career need is to identify another career and major.

Case Reflection and Chapter Overview

Monica presents a very rational approach to career decision making. She starts down one path and, when presented with a barrier (e.g., a disability, family disagreements), she adjusts the plan and keeps moving. This type of life adjustment or flexibility is typical of the military way of life. Monica recognizes her flexibility and uses her strengths to explore future careers. At this point in Monica's life, her first priority is to quickly set out a plan for her future with the assistance of all the benefits she has earned in her five years of active duty service. Monica's first stop was the vocational rehabilitation office at her local VA, where they paid for her education due to her shoulder disability. For Monica, knowing what was available for her as a veteran and having insight into what she wanted gave her direction and support.

Making a career decision and job searching are two important career-counseling topics for veterans. The first decision that a veteran needs to make is whether to continue in a career field similar to his or her military position(s) or to explore alternative options. As career theories provide a guide for helping individuals make career choices, we will first review how career theories apply to transitioning veterans.

Application of Career Theories

Career practitioners use career theories as a way to frame career counseling sessions. For example, the oldest approach was first offered by Frank Parsons' theory (1909), which outlines three essential steps: knowing oneself, knowing one's options (and the conditions of success in an occupation), and true reasoning to create a list of sensible options. A career practitioner applying Parsons' approach might divide the sessions into those three areas, with the first session focusing on intake, the second on career assessment results, the third on researching information, and the fourth on narrowing down and trying out options of interest.

Other career theories emphasize the interaction between a person's interest and environments (Holland, 1997; Lofquist & Dawis, 1991) by telling or constructing one's story (Savickas, 1997), personal agency and overcoming barriers (Lent, Brown, & Hackett, 1994), learning from experience (Krumboltz & Henderson, 2002), taking advantage of opportunities (Krumboltz, 2009), and addressing dysfunctional career thinking (Sampson, Reardon, Peterson, & Lenz, 2004).

Applying Cognitive Information Processing Theory to Veterans' Career Choices

While each of the theories described above might likely apply to veterans making career decisions, only one article has been written that expressly provides an application of theory to working with veterans. Clemons and Milsom (2008) described how cognitive information processing theory (CIP; Sampson et. al, 2004) could be applied to veterans' transitions into civilian work. CIP identifies four elements of an effective career decision, including self-knowledge, occupational knowledge, decision making, and metacognitions. Because these components represent common intervention points for career practitioners, the next sections are organized with these titles, followed by a section on job searching.

Self-Knowledge

Traditional inventories and nonstandardized approaches (such as card sorts or an Ideal Day exercise) can be used to help veterans assess their values, interests, and skills. A thorough review of 71 assessment tools is provided in *A Counselor's Guide to Career Assessment Instruments* (Whitfield, Feller, & Wood, 2009). This book provides details on the psychometric properties of various assessments, such as validity, reliability, the normative population for the test, adequacy of manuals, costs, and use in counseling. These are all important considerations when choosing an assessment. Assessments that might be of use would be those that assess values, interests, or skills. Standardized inventories such as the Campbell Interest and Skill Survey, Self-Directed Search, SDS and Strong Interest Inventory, Kuder Career Search or non-standardized approaches such as card sorts,

an ideal day activity, or the career story interview (Savickas, 1989) might be useful assessments.

The ASVAB is a test that all military personnel must complete before entering the military. The ASVAB program also contains an inventory modeled on the Self-Directed Search, called Find Your Interests (FYI) that yields a Holland RIASEC code. There is also a section in the program on work-related values. This information may provide a useful baseline of client information, but the career practitioner should ask if the veteran's interests have changed or if the veteran would be interested in taking additional assessments. Monica's FYI code when she entered the Army was IRE. The career practitioner showed Monica the descriptors of the six Holland types and asked her to guess where her interests were at this point. She said, "I think my top three types are EIR." Because her current estimates were similar to the code she had at the time of entering the military, Monica and the career practitioner made the decision not to take the Self-Directed Search at this time, but instead to explore her values.

To do this, the career practitioner created a table based on the values list on the AS-VAB website (http://asvabprogram.com/index.cfm?fuseaction=learn.workvalues) that allowed Monica to compare her values from then to now.

It's easy to see that Monica's values have remained fairly consistent over time. Challenge, creativity, and helping others are still among her primary values. What is interesting is the emer-

MOST PREFERRED		LEAST PREFERRED	
THEN (When I entered the Army)	**NOW**	**THEN**	**NOW**
1. Challenge	1. Challenge	7. Independence	7. Physical Activity
2. Helping Others	2. Creativity	8. Income	8. Security
3. Physical Activity	3. Helping Others	9. Security	9. Making or Fixing Things
4. Creativity	4. Independence	10. Public Contact	10. Public Contact
5. Variety	5. Income	11. Making or Fixing Things	11. Prestige
6. Working in a Group	6. Variety	12. Prestige	12. Working in a Group

gence of independence and income, which may be due in part to the transitions in her personal and professional life. The career practitioner could start by asking, "Monica, what do you notice about your values?" and also spend time discussing what the important values mean to her, how they were fostered in the military, and how she ideally would like to see them playing out in her work and life. It might also be useful to discuss the movement of some of the values, such as working in a group, which moved from being somewhat important to least on the list.

To work on transferable skills, a career practitioner could use a skills card sort such as the *Knowdell Motivated Skills Card Sort,* in which the client sorts cards of skills into piles according to motivation to and proficiency of use, to identify which skills are most developed and most preferred. Monica's highest rated skills are listed below.

Another approach would be to list critical skills that employers want, such as communication skills, analytical skills, technological literacy, problem-solving skills, interpersonal skills (including

working with diverse individuals or teamwork), leadership and management abilities, and planning or organizational skills. Afterwards, the counselor could ask the veteran to talk about examples and experiences that demonstrate those critical skills. The career practitioner created the table below and had Monica complete it between sessions.

The table was useful in building Monica's confidence in talking with employers about her abilities, and also highlighted where she needed to gain experience.

A strengths-based approach (Schutt, 2007) is a tool to help clients identify "seeds of excellence" within themselves, and then create "images of excellence" that they can use as visual goals to accomplish. When Monica's career practitioner asked her to describe a time when she was the happiest in her career, when she was performing well and enjoying her work, Monica described the following situation: "When I was promoted to sergeant, I was given a task that few soldiers felt comfortable doing. I was to train others with Soviet weapons and be responsible for their accountability." Following

Skills I am Highly Motivated to Use	Skills I am Highly Proficient at Using
	Solving Mathematical Probldems Speaking/Interpreting Foreign Languages Problem Solving Training Others

Critical Skills Employers Desire	My Examples and Experiences That Demonstrate the Skills
Communication	I enjoy giving presentations.
Analytical	I'm good with numbers and am a systematic thinker.
Technological Literacy	I know my way around a computer.
Problem-Solving	I live to solve problems.
Interpersonal (including working of teams and with diverse individuals)	I like working with others in a team approach.
Leadership/Management	I attained rank very fast and am a good leader.
Organizational	I work best when I am organized.

this description, Monica and her career practitioner identified themes of perseverance, challenge, and assertiveness. Monica's career practitioner then asked her to visualize herself back during that time, when she was performing well and enjoying her work, and to create an image that would remind her of that positive experience. Monica decided on a picture of her team because she said it reminded her of her challenge, team members, and their success. They then discussed the specific strengths that Monica was demonstrating during that time when she was at her very best. Monica identified the following strengths of loving a challenge, being assertive, and tenacious. Based on this exploration, they began to visualize Monica's ideal work place, one in which she could use her strengths and talents. This discussion also helped when Monica began interviewing for positions, as she was able to better evaluate how well a potential job or work environment would fit with her unique strengths.

A military-familiar tool would be the DD Form 214, which provides a transcript of the person's service given upon leaving the military. The career practitioner can ask the veteran to refer to the form and describe in detail his or her military experiences, achievements, roles, and responsibilities (Clemons & Milsom, 2008). This would be similar to how a career practitioner might use a person's resume or work history to identify transferable skills. A portion of Monica's DD Form 214 is below.

The DD Form 214 document should be used as a starting place, with the understanding that in many instances the military provides on-the-job-training that is not included on the DD214. Jobs that were relevant to other units but not assigned are also not always included on the form. Best practice would encourage the veteran to share all the "jobs" he or she has had. In reviewing Monica's DD214 form, the career practitioner asked her to describe each occupation and commendation. They listed the skills that were required for each job and then starred those that Monica enjoyed using most (see below). When Monica had trouble listing skills for one of her jobs, the career practitioner went to http://vetsuccess.gov/military_skills_translators, entered the military job title, and found skills to

PRIMARY SPECIALTY (List number, title and years and months in speciality. List additional speciality numbers and titles involving periods of one or more years). 51G20 CONSTRUCTION ENGINEER – 3 YRS MOS//NOTHING FOLLOWS	RECORD OF SERVICE	YEAR(S)	MONTH(S)	DAY(S)
	a. DATE ENTERED AD* THIS PERIOD	2004	11	04
	b. SEPARATION DATE THIS PERIOD	2007	11	04
	c. NET ACTIVE SERVICE THIS PERIOD	0003	0	0
	d. TOTAL PRIOR ACTIVE SERVICE	0000	0	
	e. TOTAL PRIOR INACTIVE SERVICE	0000	00	00
	f. FOREIGN SERVICE	0000	00	00
	g. SEA SERVICE	0000	00	00
	h. EFFECTIVE DATE OF PAY GRADE	2004	11	04
Decorations, Medals, Badges, Citations and Campaign Ribbons Awarded or Authorized //Army Commendatioin Medal//Army Achievement Medal (3dr Award)//Army Good Conduct Medal// National Defense Service Medal//NOTHING FOLLOWS	**MILITARY EDUCATION** (Course title, number of weeks, and month and year completed) Soils Analyst, 8 WEEKS, JAN 2005//NOTHING FOLLOWS *AD means Active Duty			

Jobs Held	Skills Used (* skills I prefer using)
Soils Analyst	*Math, *science, *working outside
Linguist	Spanish and *Russian language and * training
TV Playback Specialist	Following a schedule and working alone

add to the list. Another approach would be to ask Monica to generate a list of skills and attributes used in performance evaluations, training records, and productive activities, and use these keywords in O*NET to generate options.

Knowledge About Options

Knowledge about options consists of occupational knowledge and educational or training options. Occupational knowledge consists of facts about specific occupations as well as schemas for organizing the information. Veterans likely know most about occupations within the military; thus, helping build occupational knowledge about civilian occupations will be necessary and may require significant research time. Tools used with the general population, such as the O*NET and the *Online Occupational Handbook,* will also be useful for transitioning military.

However, there are specific tools that might be more useful for this group. For example, O*NET has a crosswalk between military and civilian occupations (http://www.onetonline.org/crosswalk/MOC/) that would be useful for a veteran interested in finding a civilian occupation similar to the military job(s) she or he held. However, it is not always the case that a veteran is looking for something similar. As in Monica's case, upon leaving the military, she was ready to do something quite different.

There is often more than one educational or training route for a specific career, but some options are more straightforward. For example, people wanting to be nurses or engineers must study nursing or engineering, respectively. However, the majority of careers don't have a direct match with a specific major, which can be liberating, overwhelming, or both. If a clear career is in mind, the individual can explore the different possible training and experience paths that might lead to successful employment in that area. One option for

identifying possible majors or fields of study is to use the *Educational Opportunities Finder* (Rosen, Holmberg, & Holland, 1994), which uses Holland codes to generate educational or training options.

In addition to identifying a major or field of study, there is also the decision of how much training to get and where to get it. Depending on the civilian career goal and how close it is to the veteran's military training and work, the training needed might range from a certificate to a graduate degree. Options might include vocational education, apprenticeships, continuing education, volunteering, and post-secondary degrees ranging from associate's degrees to doctorates. The decision on where to get the education and training is a very important one, and the career practitioner can be helpful by sharing how to evaluate programs and schools. There are many unethical groups that are more than willing to take money that a veteran has earned towards education only to provide a certificate or degree that is useless or not valued in industry or by other education providers. A career practitioner should encourage the veteran to research all training options to ensure that the provider is accredited by a nationally accepted regional accreditation body.

Two useful websites for researching accreditations are the Database of Accredited Postsecondary Institutions and Programs (http://ope.ed.gov/accreditation/) and the U.S. Department of Education's page on regional and national institutional accrediting agencies (http://www2.ed.gov/admins/finaid/accred/accreditation_pg6.html). Career practitioners should also be aware of the Service members Opportunity College (SOC) Consortium (http://www.dantes.doded.mil/Sub%20Pages/Higher_Ed/HigherEd_SOC.html), which consists of about 1,800 colleges that allow military members to transfer credits and count military experience for credit across the schools in the

	Accreditation?	Degree?	Length?	Cost?
Training Option A				
Training Option B				

consortium. Because military members may move around extensively, this can be a barrier to earning a postsecondary degree, but this consortium removes that barrier.

Providing a checklist for evaluating education and training options might decrease the chances of this happening. A sample is included above. The veteran could add other columns that are of specific interest, such as distance learning, location, class size, who employs graduates, graduation rate, and so forth.

Another potentially useful tool for veterans wanting to pursue their education is Veterans Upward Bound (www.navub.org), which offers academic preparation, refresher courses, tutoring, mentoring, assistance with applications for admission, financial aid, GI Bill, and scholarships. It also offers academic advising, career counseling, and referrals to other community agencies that serve veterans. A career practitioner working with veterans should make a connection with this office, which can be easily done through the state VUB locator on the website.

Sources of Education Funding

Veterans may also be interested in learning about different ways to finance their education. In addition to financial aid that is available to all U.S. citizens, veterans also have access to benefits due to their military service. The most common include the Montgomery GI (MGI) Bill, the Post-9/11 GI Bill, and the VEAP/REAP programs. A brief description of each is provided on page 23.

Decision Making (CASVE Cycle)

As the knowledge domains begin to grow, the veteran will begin applying that information to the career decision. CIP theory outlines five phases in a decision making model, called the CASVE Cycle.

The ***Communication*** phase involves identifying the gap between where the client is and where he or she would like to be, and exploring internal and external pressures to make a choice. The ***Analysis*** phase involves building self and/or occupational knowledge. ***Synthesis*** consists of elaborating options based on self-knowledge and then narrowing those options down into a reasonable number, usually three to five. ***Valuing*** includes an evaluation of the pros and cons of each option for self, significant others, and family, resulting in a prioritized list. ***Execution*** is the implementation of the first choice, followed by ***Communication-Revisited,*** to determine if the gap still exists.

The career practitioner presented Monica with a client version of the CASVE Cycle (available at http://www.career.fsu.edu/documents/cognitive%20information/%20processing/What%20Involved%20in%20Career%20Choice.html). A summary of her progress through the cycle is presented below.

Monica's CASVE Cycle *(See chart on p. 24)*

Metacognitions

This domain houses self-talk, which influences the other three areas in the Pyramid of Information Processing Domains. Dysfunctional career thinking (such as "No one is ever going to hire me," or "There are no jobs that interest me") can get in the way of making a career decision. If mental health needs are significant enough or if suicidal thoughts are present, the career practitioner should address these first (either through focusing on those concerns if qualified or referring to a professional practitioner). Usually, a career practitioner can pick up on the presence of these negative thoughts as the veteran is speaking during the conversation. Depending on the intensity or frequency of

Comparison of MGI, Post 9/11 GI and VEAP/REAP

Montgomery GI Bill	The MGI Bill allows for up to 36 months of educational benefits. Enrollees pay $100 per month for months and must complete a minimum service obligation. Extra contributions ("buying up") can significantly increase the stipend for attending school fulltime. MGIB-SR program may be available for members of the selected reserve. Reservists who are actively drilling and have a 6-year obligation in the selected reserve are eligible for the Montgomery GI Bill benefits.	http://www.gibill.va.gov/benefits/ montgomery_gibill/index.html
Post-9/11 GI Bill	Provides up to 36 months of financial support for education and housing for individuals with at least 90 days of aggregate service on or after 9/11/01 (including National Guard after 10/1/11), or individuals discharged with a service-connected disability after 30 days	http://www.gibill.va.gov/benefits/ post_911_givill/index.html
REAP	Reserve Educational Assistance Program: contribution-based programs to provide service members with educational funding benefits.	http://www.gibill.va.gov/benefits/ other_programs/reap.html
VEAP	Veterans Educational Assistance Program: contribution-based programs to provide service members with educational funding benefits, for those who entered service for the first time between January 1, 1977, and June 30, 1985.	http://www/gibill.va.gov/benefits/ other_programs/veap.html

these types of remarks, the career practitioner may want to introduce an assessment such as the Career Thoughts Inventory (Sampson, Peterson, Lenz, Reardon, & Saunders, 1996), the Career Decision Scale (Osipow, Carney, Winer, Yanico, & Koeschier, 1987), the Career Beliefs Inventory (Krumboltz, 1994), or My Vocational Situation (Holland, Daiger, & Power, 1980) to identify the problem thoughts. It is possible for one negative

career thought to severely impact the process. In Monica's situation, she was very concerned about learning a new field from scratch, one that would be very different from engineering. She also had doubts about being accepted into programs because of her age and being a veteran.

If the career practitioner does not have access to one of these standardized tools, a nonstandardized tool that might be of help is the Career Deci-

Communication	Gap: Between leaving a career in engineering and considering a medical career, but not exactly sure External Cues: Family pressures, financial, impending divorce Internal Cues: Stress to find "something", fear of leaving the Army
Analysis	Interests: Enterprising, Investigative, Realistic Values: Challenge, Creativity, Helping Others, Independence, Income Skills: Current Options: Pre-med Knowledge About Options: Researched the course to be studied in order to go pre-med
Synthesis	Elaboration: Other fields that may help to get to medical school: science careers, psychology, nursing, occupational therapy Crystallization: Nurse Anesthetist, Psychologist, and Scientist

Valuing	Option 1: Psychology:
	    Pros: Helping the patient mentally not just physically
	    Cons: Many more years of school and may not be a clinician
	Option 2: Medical school
	    Pros: Working with the human body and helping people in need
	    Cons:

Execution	She worked as a respiratory therapist in her local hospital, and she had first-hand experience on taking care of patients and their needs.
Communication – Revisited	Gap: After she had this exierence, she felt that the gap had closed. Internal Cues: Peace, happy, "knowing" she was doing the right thing. External Cues: Positive feedback from instructors and employer, that she was in the right field.

sion Space Worksheet (career.fsu.edu/techcenter/FCDA/2012/DecisionSpaceWorksheet.doc). Monica listed the following as "thoughts, feelings, circumstances, people, or events" that were bearing on her career decision: (1) fear of leaving the Army, (2) finding a job, (3) taking care of her daughter, (4) issues with her husband, (5) reaching out to friends, (6) issues with money, (7) transportation problems to the college town, (8) fear of the unknown, (9) understanding college life, and (10) feeling too old for a new career. Her completed worksheet shown at right.

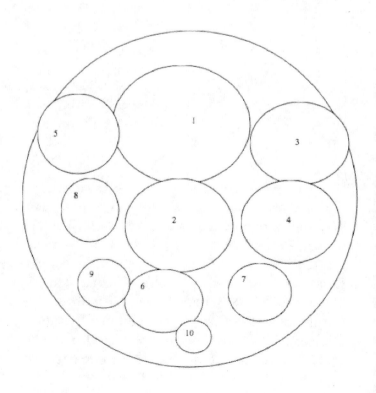

Monica's Completed Decision Space Worksheet:

There are many ways in which a person might complete the Decision Space Worksheet. Usually, the list of pressures in step one is a randomized list of concerns, and during the second step (visually representing the concerns) the magnitude and relationship of each concern becomes clear. In Monica's case, it seems that the brainstormed list and the visual representation are in exact order. The most pressing concern to Monica is her fear of leaving the Army. Following that, concerns two, three, and four are about equal in concern. When questioned about those that were connected versus those that were standing alone, she indicated that there was no additional meaning to that — but the career practitioner held this in mind during future sessions (i.e., that some concerns were more closely connected than others).

Career Readiness

Career readiness has been defined by Sampson et al. (2004, p. 68) as "the capacity of an individual to make appropriate career choices while taking into account the complexity of family, social, economic, and organizational factors that influence an individual's career development." These theorists identify two dimensions that comprise readiness: capability and complexity. Most individuals will come to counseling when they get to the point that something needs to change, and they realize they need some help making that happen. They may feel "ready" to make a change immediately and hope for a quick fix or answer, not realizing that there may be other issues (i.e., in this theory, capability, and complexity issues) that might need to be addressed first. Some of these complexities were outlined as mental health challenges in Chapter 1 and as transition concerns in Chapter 2.

Monica appears to be capable of making a career decision. She has made complex decisions in the past and is able to hold multiple, sometimes contrasting viewpoints in her mind, weigh pros and cons, and make an effective choice. With the present decision, there appears to be some dysfunctional career thinking and some negativity that might be impacting her ability to choose. Monica often questioned her ability to secure a job in the civilian world because she was not sure if the "civilian world" had changed while she was on active duty. She also questioned if civilians would want

to hire her with her VA disability. The complexity of Monica's life is what is likely having the greatest impact on her decision situation. Her marriage, her daughter, financial concerns, and finding employment are all adding pressure to her decision. The combined capability and complexity issues would place Monica in the "moderately ready" category, suggesting that she will need brief-assisted help from a career practitioner or specialist, who will help Monica keep the negative thoughts in check and also pay attention to the contextual issues impacting Monica's decision.

Individual Career Learning Plan

The purpose of an Individual Career Learning Plan (ICLP) is to create a collaborative document that identifies co-constructed goals, activities to meet these goals, time required for each activity and the priority of each activity. The ICLP can be especially useful when there is more than one goal. For example, a veteran may have the following goals: see which civilian occupations match my interests and skills, see what civilian jobs I might easily be qualified for based on my military experience, and update my resume. Some of the activities might be taking career assessments, using O*NET, using DD Form 214, and reviewing sample resumes (Clemons & Milsom, 2008).

The concept of an ICLP is likely to be known to the veteran because the Transition Assistance Program (TAP; turbotap.org) developed by the Department of Defense uses a similar form, the *Individual Transition Plan* (ITP). TAP suggests using DD Form 2648 (*Pre-Separation Counseling Checklist*) as an outline for completing the ITP. A sample is included in Appendix B. Not every service member may have taken advantage of the TAP program, but using this form may help the discussion about career transition. This form uses language familiar to the veteran and can then serve as a springboard for talking about transferable skills, career options, and resume writing.

Towards the end of Monica's initial session, the career practitioner worked with her to create the ICLP presented on the next page.

Individual Career Learning Plan

Goal: #1: <u>Choose a career that matches my interests</u>

Goal: #2: <u>Find a major that corresponds to the career I want</u>

Goal: #3: <u>Find a job</u>

Activity	Purpose / Outcome	Estimated Time	Goal #
Review	Identify skills areas	1 hour	1
Complete interest inventory	See interests and related occupations	1 hour	2
Use O*NET and other online information sources	See occupations related to interests; learn which majors might feed into that degree	1 – 4 hours	3
Attend job search workshop	Improve job search strategies	1 hour	5
Review list of majors	See what majors are available	30 minutes	4

As the sessions continued, they adjusted the ICLP, moving some items to occur sooner and making additional items. The ICLP helped impose a structure on what had seemed like an overwhelming process, and broke it into more manageable steps. Also, because it was co-created, the control was clearly in Monica's hand.

The preceding sections have discussed the components of making a career decision through the lens of a career theory (cognitive information processing theory). The other main career concern is how to locate, apply, and interview for positions. We will be covering these topics in the following section.

Job Searching

Job searching is another key concern for transitioning veterans that comprises several elements, including creating a cover letter and resume, identifying potential positions and employers, networking, interviewing, negotiating job offers, and learning about specific job search strategies. For the veteran, each of these may pose unique challenges. In addition, there is always the concern of how military experience will be perceived by employers. If a veteran is in the reserve, there may be an added concern of how a potential employer will view someone who may be called for duty for months at a time. Career practitioners and specialists are well versed in job search tools and strategies. The goal of this section is not to rehash what is already known, but to provide veteran-specific information, issues, strategies, and suggestions on the areas of resume writing, locating jobs, and interviewing.

Resume Writing

One of the major difficulties veterans may face is translating their military experience into civilian terms. Describing what an "Assault Boat Coxswain" does and then relating that to civilian work may require some discussion in counseling. The veteran's DD Form 214 might be a useful place to start a resume. In addition, a career practitioner can use online searches to see specific job descriptions to enhance the resume. For example, a search on "NEC BM-0164 Assault Box Coxswain" yielded this description from one site: "Handles and beaches landing craft in assault waves. Supervises boat crew in hoisting and lowering operations. Handles all types of cargo including stowing in boat. Assists in salvage operation." (http://usmilitary.about.com/od/navynecs/p/BM0164.html). From this description, certain words come to mind — manage, direct, supervise — that are very transferable and will be of interest to employers. Seeing sample resumes for careers of interest will help the veteran become familiar with what employers are looking for, and help him or her learn about common words and descriptions used. In addition to this, the career practitioner will want to advise the veteran against using too many acronyms or military jargon, as well as to leave out specific details about active combat. The emphasis should be on the value that being a veteran adds, as demonstrated through dedication, sacrifice for the greater good, persistence, team player, reliability, strong work ethic, and so forth.

Locating Jobs

Another important aspect of job searching is connecting the veteran with employers. In addition to identifying employers who are likely to hire for certain positions, it is important to point veterans to websites and employers who are specifically interested in hiring veterans. Many of these are listed in Appendix C, but there are also many resources on the topic such as *Career Planning and the Internet* (Osborn, Dikel, & Sampson, 2011), *Internet Your Way to a New Job* (Doyle, 2011), *Job Hunting Online* (Bolles & Bolles, 2011), and *The Panic-Free Job Search: Unleash the Power of the Web and Social Networking to Get Hired* (Hill, 2012). There are also Career One Stops in all 50 states, and each of these has a "Vet Rep" (see http://www.taonline.com/VetReps/SearchVetReps.asp).

A common job search strategy is to utilize a person's network to identify work opportunities. However, because persons in the military may be required to relocate frequently, a stable network might not exist (Drummet, Coleman & Cable, 2003). Thus, a career practitioner may need to help the veteran develop and use networks for job searching, including social networking sites. One option that Monica used to build her network was to explore the staffing services industry, where she "temped" in several different positions for different

employers. She also decided to do a cold call to her local hospital. She walked into the hospital, without having any experience at all in medicine, and told the respiratory therapist supervisor that she would work for free for three months in exchange for on-the-job training (assuring him that she was a very quick learner). After one month, they hired her full time. She also impressed many of the doctors who offered to sponsor her for medical school.

Interviewing

In addition to using DD Form 214, training records, performance evaluations, and citation recommendations as springboards for resume writing and skills identification, these forms can also be helpful in preparing for interviews. For interviewing, a career practitioner might consider providing the veteran with common interview questions and then practicing how to effectively integrate military experience into the answers in a way that civilians can appreciate. For example, consider the question "Tell me about a time when you had to perform under pressure." The veteran likely has ample examples, but should be coached to choose the example that can answer the question most completely, in civilian language, in the shortest amount of time. While there may be a temptation to tell the whole war story answer in 1–1½ minutes, a better approach would be for the veteran to choose an example that is most closely related to the position vacancy.

The veteran should be made aware of illegal questions, such as "So were you honorably discharged?" as well as uncomfortable questions that might be reflective of the interviewer's point of view, and work to create a reasonable response. It is also illegal to ask if a veteran or reservist is planning to take leave to serve in the military, or to ask for military service papers.

For both the resume and the interview, emphasis should be on helping the veteran frame accomplishments and stories in a personal way. This may be difficult for someone who is used to working with a team and framing all successes and failures as a team experience. Another challenge is that many enlisted military members have performed jobs in the military that in the civilian private economy would only be performed by seasoned, experienced, degreed employees. Adding to the complexity is that civilian employers may be intimidated by veterans with extensive accomplishments. Veterans have to be very strategic between taking credit and revealing their true capabilities and not being perceived as a threat to those less accomplished, older, or in management positions. In our experience, many veterans need a significant amount of coaching about taking credit for their contributions while balancing that with "bragimony" (braggadocio). Striking a balance can be a challenge.

Some of the interview questions that most concerned Monica included:

- Please share some of your personal accomplishments.
- Describe a time when you stood out of the work group.
- Describe a time you decided not to follow the orders of a superior.
- Under what conditions would you consider not following orders?
- Describe a time you broke the rules and why?

The career practitioner worked with Monica to determine what was behind these questions, what was behind the concerns, and then finding answers to the questions. During one session, they role-played an interview to build confidence in her ability to answer the questions.

Finding Credentialed Career Service Providers

With so many companies and individuals offering to "help" veterans for a fee or free, online or in person, it can be an overwhelming process to select a service provider. Information on how to find and select quality career service providers would likely be helpful for veterans. Also, some of our profession's terminology, such as the difference between practitioner, coach, advisor, counselor, specialist, or/and credentials such as NCC or GCDF might be confusing to a veteran. This information could be provided on a website or as a handout. An ex-

ample on how to choose a qualified practitioner is available at NCDA "Guidelines for Choosing a Counselor" (http://associationdatabase.com/aws/NCDA/pt/sp/consumer_choose).

Case Study Closure

Monica's story is a fairly common one with transitioning military. The career issue was determining what civilian career she wanted to pursue and the education/training necessary to achieve that goal. She was very capable of making a career decision, but the complexities of her situation complicated the decision and necessitated the use of a career practitioner. In this chapter, we demonstrated how a career practitioner can couple tools and resources that are common in career service delivery with military forms that the veteran may have. We demonstrated how career theory supports career practice by applying cognitive information processing theory to Monica's case. Many of the specific interventions would be supported by other career theories as well.

Monica's self-knowledge had changed slightly. Her interests remained in the same areas, but her prioritized values had shifted. She had some negative career thinking that impacted her ability to see her skills and her future options clearly, and also impacted her emotionally when preparing for interviews. The career practitioner focused on both career needs as well as the mental health issues related to anxiety to help Monica move forward with her choice. By working through the CASVE Cycle, Monica was able to select an option that was related to being a doctor (in this case, respiratory therapist) but more easily attainable given her other life demands.

Summary

Many of the career counseling topics of interest to veterans are similar to the topics of interest to the general public. CIP theory would state that knowledge about self, options, decision-making, and awareness/monitoring of self-talk are the general components that should be covered in a career counseling session. However, working with veterans requires knowledge of other tools designed especially for them that can enhance the career decision-making or job-search process. Asking the veteran to elaborate on military achievements and experiences; using forms such as DD Form 214, training records, performance evaluations, and citation recommendations; and incorporating veteran websites such as those listed in this chapter are three practical tools a career practitioner can use with this population.

References

Bolles, R. N., & Bolles, M. E. (2011). *Job hunting online.* Berkeley, CA: Ten Speed Press.

Clemons, E. V., & Milsom, A. S. (2008). Enlisted service members' transition into the civilian world of work: A cognitive information processing approach. *The Career Development Quarterly, 56,* 246–255.

Doyle, A. (2011). *Internet your way to a new job.* Cupertina, CA: Happy About.

Drummet, A. R., Coleman, M., & Cable, S. (2003). Military families under stress: Implications for family life education. *Family Relations, 52,* 279–287.

Hill, P. (2012). *The panic-free job search: Unleash the power of the web and social networking to get hired.* Pompton Plains, NJ: Career Press, Inc.

Holland, J. L. (1997). *Making vocational choices: A theory of vocational personalities and work environments* (3rd ed.). Odessa, FL: Psychological Assessment Resources, Inc.

Holland, J. L., Daiger, D. C, & Power, P. G. (1980). *My Vocational Situation.* Palo Alto, CA: Consulting Psychologists Press.

Krumboltz, J. D. (1994). The Career Beliefs Inventory. *Journal of Counseling & Development, 72,* 424-428.

Krumboltz, J. D. (2009). The Happenstance Learning theory. *Journal of Career Assessment, 17,* 135–154. DOI: 10.1177/1069072708328861

Krumboltz, J. D., & Henderson, S. J. (2002). A learning theory for career counselors. In S. G. Niles (Ed.), *Adult career development: Concepts, issues and practices* (3rd ed., pp. 41–58). Tulsa, OK: National Career Development Association.

Lent, R.W., Brown, S.D., & Hackett, G. (1994). Toward a unifying social cognitive theory of career and academic interest, choice, and performance. *Journal of Vocational Behavior, 45,* 79–122.

Lofquist, L. H., & Dawis, R. V. (1991). *Essentials of person-environment-correspondence counseling.* Minneapolis, MN: University of Minnesota Press.

Osborn, D. S., Dikel, M. R., & Sampson, J. P., Jr. (2011). *The Internet: A guide to using the Internet in career planning* (3rd Ed.). Broken Arrow, OK: National Career Development Association.

Osipow, S. H., Carney, C. G., Winer, J. L., Yanico, B. J., & Koeschier, M. (1987). *Career Decision Scale* (3rd rev.). Odessa, FL: Psychological Assessment Resources.

Parsons, F. (1909). *Choosing a vocation.* Boston: Houghton Mifflin.

Rosen, D., Holmberg, K., & Holland, J. L. (1994). The educational opportunities finder. Odessa, FL: Psychological Assessment Resources.

Sampson, J. P., Jr., Peterson, G. W., Lenz, J. G., Reardon, R. C, & Saunders, D. E. (1996). *The Career Thoughts Inventory.* Odessa, FL: Psychological Assessment Resources.

Sampson, J.P. Jr., Reardon, R.C., Peterson, G.W., & Lenz, J. G. (2004). *Career counseling and services: A cognitive information processing approach.* Pacific Grove, CA: Brooks/Cole.

Savickas, M. L. (1989). Career-style assessment and counseling. In T. Sweeney (Ed.), *Adlerian counseling: A practicalapproach for a new decade* (3rd ed., pp. 289–320). Muncie, IN: Accelerated Development Press.

Savickas, M. L. (1997). Career adaptability: An integrative construct for Life-Span, Life-Space theory. *The Career Development Quarterly, 45,* 247-259.

Schutt, D. A., Jr. (2007). *Strength-based approach to career development using appreciative inquiry.* Broken Arrow, OK: National Career Development Association.

Whitfield, E. A., Feller, R. W., & Wood, C. (Eds.). (2009). *A Counselor's Guide to Career Assessment Instruments* (5th ed.). Broken Arrow, OK: National Career Development Association.

Case Study

Steve is currently active-duty military in the Army and has recently began receiving intensive inpatient comprehensive treatment for a mild traumatic brain injury related to his service. Steve is married with two young children and is far from his family while he receives treatment. There has been tension within Steve's marriage as his wife was struggling with situations in which symptoms related to his injury (such as his memory problems) have created issues within the family. Prior to his injury, Steve planned to make a career of the military and transition out after completing 20 years of service, allowing him to receive full retirement benefits. Steve served as a pilot of a CH-47 helicopter that crashed in Afghanistan. The whole crew survived, but Steve suffered an injury when his head slammed against the side of the cockpit upon touching down. Though he did not possess an overt wound on his head, Steve sensed something was not right when he began having issues with remembering various instructions on preparing for flights that he had no issue with prior to the crash. Steve went to the doctor on base who determined he should not fly until he has been fully evaluated. Steve has been identified as having a mild traumatic brain injury and was referred to a comprehensive treatment facility for rehabilitation.

Part of his treatment has been to receive career counseling, which occurred off-site at a local university's career center. Steve's wife, Ally, indicated being supportive of his treatment, but is concerned about ensuring the children's well-being during his recovery. Though Ally has experience being the sole care-giver for the children, she expected Steve to assume some of this responsibility upon his return from deployment. Ally did not anticipate the lengthy absence associated with Steve's recovery and has expressed frustration with feeling as though she is again the sole care-giver for their children.

Steve has begun meeting with a career practitioner to explore options for him going forward. Steve was unsure if he will be medically discharged or if he will continue in the Army. Though he has expressed being unhappy about the potential for him not being able to fly helicopters, he was interested in exploring options related to his interests.

Reflections on Case Study

While the specific details of Steve's circumstance may be unique, Steve's situation is not uncommon. People in the military often encounter significant issues related to their service in the military that require them to reconsider their career aspirations and goals. The career practitioner addressing Steve's concerns would benefit from having a foundational knowledge of the current career challenges facing military personnel and veterans with issues stemming from their service in addition to useful interventions to assist these individuals.

Military Personnel and Disabilities

This chapter will discuss providing career counseling to veteran with various disabilities. Given the issues within our military population related to recent military engagements in Iraq and Afghanistan, it is important to examine ways in which career practitioners providing career services can assist these individuals. As stated in Chapter 2 on transitions, this process can be difficult, requiring a thoughtful approach to assisting military personnel who may be leaving the military.

For the purposes of attending to the current and future issues presented to career practitioners serving this population, the focus will be on psychological and physical injuries related to experience in the field as opposed to preexisting conditions or disabilities not incurred from military involvement. This is not intended to minimize preexisting considerations, but to instruct career practitioners of methods to address the primary concerns of military personnel with service-related disabilities. This chapter will provide an overview of service-related physical and psychological disabilities within the military population, the relevance of career counseling when working with military personnel and veterans with disabilities, and the use of cognitive information processing theory (Sampson, Reardon, Peterson, & Lenz, 2004) combined with a strength-based approach to address career development issues.

Current Landscape of Military Engagement

While specific details of situations may differ, Steve's career concern born out of his combat related injury is not unique. Before examining various aspects of career development in military personnel and veterans with disabilities, it is important to understand the broader context of recent military conflicts. There have been roughly 1.7 million troops deployed to Operations Enduring Freedom and Iraqi Freedom (OEF/OIF; Berger, 2010). While exposure to combat is in itself a significant experience, the recent engagements have been unique in that the psychological wounds of war currently outstrip the physical injuries related to military experience (Sammons & Batten, 2008). Some estimates indicate roughly 30% of military personnel will exhibit demonstrable pathology related to their service with post-traumatic stress disorder (PTSD) being frequently exhibited (Sammons & Batten). In addition to psychological issues, traumatic brain injury (TBI) is characterized as the signature wound of these conflicts (Bagalman, 2011). There are also high numbers of active duty military and veterans with various injuries such as loss of limbs, blindness, hearing loss, and disfigurement (Marchione, 2012).

While both physical and psychological disabilities present challenges to military personnel and veterans, a combination of disorders can create a unique constellation of co-morbid injuries affecting career development (Collins & Kennedy, 2008). In terms of the magnitude of the current number of those who may be disabled, there appears to be a significant increase in veterans applying for disabilities, with roughly 45% of veterans seeking compensation for alleged service-related injuries (Marchione, 2012). The career development of those afflicted is a needed area of focus for career practitioners.

Career Counseling

As indicated in Steve's situation, there are several dimensions in need of attention on the part of his career practitioner. In the initial interview, Steve states, "I am trying to figure out my options. I thought I could continue flying helicopters, but it doesn't seem like that is going to work out. Where does that leave me?" Steve indicates a sincere desire to continue in his current occupation, but he may be unable to do this because of his injury. This element of complexity adds depth to his career concerns requiring the career practitioner to consider multiple factors, such as grief over the loss of his identity and occupation, anxiety over an uncertain future, and the need for hope in his potential to actively engage in his career development.

Many military personnel have entered the military with the thought of making this a permanent career. Certain injuries such as TBI can be tangible barriers to continuing in their current occupations within the military to the point that many must consider early retirement and transition to civilian work. Being aware of this potential reality is an important element of career counseling with military personnel and veterans with disabilities.

When assisting military personnel with disabilities, career counseling offers an intervention capable of positively impacting several facets of their functioning. Career counseling has been found to have a tangible benefit for those with TBI (Keyser-Marcus et al., 2002). Reducing depression, the likelihood of substance abuse, and other secondary deleterious outcomes are often side effects of addressing career issues (Wehman, Targett, West, & Kregel, 2005). This speaks to the interconnected nature of mental health and career concerns on someone's overall well-being. Related to Steve's presenting problem, addressing his career concern has the potential to improve his emotional health and alleviate familial stress. We will further examine a few approaches designed to assist with issues of career attainment.

Cognitive Information Processing Approach

Chapter 3 provides a functional level of information regarding cognitive information processing theory (CIP). As a reminder, CIP is designed to help clients make an appropriate current career choice and, in the process, learn improved problem-solving and decision-making skills which can be utilized in future choices (Sampson, Reardon, Peterson, & Lenz, 2004). The elements of *knowing* about a career choice and *doing* in regards to engaging a career concern are interconnected elements of this approach.

Due to Steve's injury and this potential feeling of disempowerment related to unfilled career expectations, counseling to enhance his sense of self-efficacy related to career problem-solving would be helpful both now and in the future. The CIP focus on affect, process, and self-determination would provide an especially useful method for assisting Steve in his career choice. In addition to CIP, strength-based counseling offers a useful adjunctive theory to enhance hope for a fulfilling future. Before fully addressing Steve's situation, it is important to provide some foundational knowledge about strength-based career counseling.

Strength-Based Career Counseling (SBCC)

Given career counseling's apparent benefit for military personnel and veterans with disabilities, it is important to examine methods for addressing these complex issues. In Steve's situation, he encountered a system intended to remediate the limitations in functioning. Prior to receiving comprehensive treatment, Steve indicated he had seen a few doctors who informed him he would probably not be able to fly helicopters again. Steve also shared that his wife had become irritated with his struggles with memory, stating that "Ally called the other day irritated that I did not remember to call the children before their first day of school. I tried to apologize and explain that my memory is just not what it used to be. After talking for a

bit, she seemed to come around. I wish there was some way she could understand what I am going through." This along with other situations in Steve's current experience presented the potential for Steve to focus more on his limitations. When considering an uncertain future, it was important to provide Steve some element of hope while also finding practical and realistic career options aligned with his interests. Strength-based counseling's attention to assets and growth can enhance Steve's view of his potential for ongoing career development.

Elements of Strength-Based Career Counseling

The basis of SBCC focuses on individual, community, and societal factors that make life worth living (Seligman & Csikszentmihalyi, 2000). A strength-based approach requires the ability to change focus from problem-solving and deficit-based work to a process of examining what has been successful and is going well (Schutt, 2007). In the realm of career counseling for military personnel and veterans, a career practitioner will focus on such concepts of resilience in overcoming difficult challenges, the potential for future growth, and internal and external resources capable of further career development. As stated by Seligman, "treatment is not just fixing what is broken, it is nurturing what is best within ourselves" (1999, p.1). This foundational philosophy offers a welcome approach for persons such as Steve who may lack a sense of hope for the future due to limitations related to his injury.

Smith's (2006) review of previous literature related to SBCC theory found several basic concepts of strength-based counseling. Themes of the propositions related to this review focus on the human desire to strive towards growth, the importance of encouragement and honoring the efforts of clients, and the need for career practitioners to provide the opportunity for clients to process feelings and thoughts associated with their situation. This highlights the need for Steve's career practitioner to not solely focus on the vocational aspects of his experience, but to take a more holistic approach.

Stages of Strength-Based Career Counseling

From these propositions, a basic structure of SBCC can be established. *Stage one* involves creating a therapeutic alliance in which a foundational relationship is established to address career development. *Stage two* involves determining the nature of the injury. While SBCC focuses more on development and growth, it is important to get a firm understanding of the nature of the disability in order to effectively create realistic goals for counseling. *Stage three* examines the current and anticipated recovery from the injury, highlighting resilience and the continuum of recovery. Depending on the injury, discussing recovering as opposed to being injured can instill hope in the future. *Stage four* of SBCC examines the values, interests, and skills of the client to determining realistic career goals associated with one's abilities and interests. Various interest inventories and assessments can be used to structure this discussion. *Stage five* creates an integrated future grounded in reality.

Including Family in the Career Decision

Military personnel and their families who experience issues related to deployment comprise a significant portion of the fighting force in Iraq and Afghanistan. Married military men and women constitute 55% engaged in Operations Enduring Freedom and Iraqi Freedom. Roughly 1 million service members have children, with 48% of these having children 5 years old or younger (Office of the Deputy Under Secretary of Defense, 2005). Career practitioners working with wounded military personnel and veterans must consider the influence and impact of the career decision on family members. Viewing the current situation in the familial context acknowledges a significant factor in the career decision and enables the career practitioner to consider methods for employing family members as a positive resource moving forward. This element of the career situation underscored the need for Steve's career practitioner to fully consider the familial aspects of his planning. Any career decision will have implications within Steve's family, which should be considered moving forward.

Case Study Closure

Elements of CIP and SBCC were incorporated to address Steve's career concern. The career practitioner working with Steve began by summarizing his current situation by stating, "Steve, I understand you have suffered a mild traumatic brain injury. Based on what you have shared, it sounds like a lot of different factors are affecting your career choices now. You had a pretty clear idea of where you wanted to go in life and then circumstances beyond your control have determined that you may need to consider other career options. It seems like your injury is affecting not only your career situation, but also your relationship with your wife and children." This empathic statement laid the foundation for holistic exploration and reframes Steve's situation as an external circumstance as opposed to an internal deficiency. The career practitioner attempted to establish the therapeutic alliance by considering all aspects of his current situation. Using CIP, Steve's career practitioner created an ICLP, which is presented below.

Individual Career Learning Plan

The career practitioner then continued by obtaining a release and speaking with Steve's physician in charge of his rehabilitation to better understand current and anticipated functionality. While installation of hope for the future was critical, goals needed to be attainable and realistic. Establishing the relationship and obtaining an accurate understanding of Steve's situation were essential aspects of working successfully with Steve. Apart from the physical characteristics of Steve's situation, the career practitioner administered the Career Thoughts Inventory (CTI; Sampson, Peterson, Lenz, Rearson, & Saunders, 1996) to determine his thoughts associated with the career decision. Due to Steve's elevated score on the CTI subscales of Decision-Making Confusion, and External Conflict, it was determined Steve had low readi-

Goal: #1: <u>Determine marketable skills associated with military experience</u>

Goal: #2: <u>Enhance understanding of options related to interests, values, and skills</u>

Goal: #3: <u>Determine job options in civilian work related to helicopter pilots</u>

Activity	Purpose/Outcome	Estimated Time Commitment	Goal #
Transferable Skills Sheet	Determine transferable skills	1 hour	1
Complete interest inventory	Find jobs that match interests	1 hour	2
I will speak with doctor related to status of being medically discharged	Find if I will continue to be able to be active duty or enter civilian work force	2 hours	1, 3
Research options related to interests and skills	Find tangible opportunities tied to values and ability	4 hours	2,3

ness due to the high level of complexity of his concern. Long-term individual career counseling was recommended.

The counselor shared with Steve his results from the CTI and processed the elevated scores on the Decision-Making Confusion and External Conflict scales. The career practitioner inquired about Steve's perceptions of the results and discussed how specific items Steve indicated a strong agreement with related to his decision-making confusion and external conflict. Steve's response was, "Yeah, that makes sense. I am unsure of how to even begin this process. In the military, decisions of what I did were made by someone else. I don't have a lot of experience with having to make a decision about my career. I also have some stuff going on at home with my wife that adds to the problem." The career practitioner then stated, "Steve, it seems you have a fair amount of things associated with this decision, such as issues with not having confidence or knowledge in making the decision in addition to the issues at home. Before we get too far into enhancing your knowledge of self and options, what do you think about completing some exercises in the CTI workbook that deals with some of these other concerns?" Steve agreed to complete prior to the next session the first three sections of the workbook, which involved him identifying and changing negative metacognitions.

Due to the need to ensure continuity of care,

Steve's career practitioner asked Steve if he could speak with other service providers who were working with Steve. After Steve provided proper consent via exchange of information forms, the career practitioner then discussed Steve's recovery process with various service providers, such as the physician overseeing his rehabilitation and his occupational therapist, in an attempt to coordinate efforts designed to support Steve in his recovery. Other service providers shared their perceptions that Steve may not be able to fly helicopters due to his mild TBI, but he could still perform fairly complicated tasks and that his memory issues had a high potential for improvement resulting from his process of rehabilitation. After consulting with service providers, the career practitioner shared the information with Steve, emphasizing the potential for growth and the uncertainty related to his ability to continue in his role in the military. Emphasizing growth and acknowledging his recovery process served to enhance hope for the future and set realistic expectations tied to current circumstances. These were simultaneously processed during the career counseling sessions.

As the career practitioner and Steve talked, they both agreed that Steve was lacking in awareness of his options related to his interests. The career practitioner gave Steve the choice of completing an interest inventory or using a computer-assisted career guidance system. Steve decided he wanted to begin with the Self-Directed Search (SDS). This decision was also associated with Steve being in the Analysis phase of his CASVE cycle. Steve's SDS results identified him as having several occupational options associated with engineering and mechanical repair. Steve shared he has always enjoyed building and repairing cars, specifically enjoying developing solutions to problems presented when engaged in the process.

A specific discussion regarding the Valuing and Execution stages of the CASVE Cycle occurred with the career practitioner processing aspects of this process, such as determine how options fit within Steve's values. Based on the previously indicated familial stress associated with his injury and the common issues associated with TBI (such as memory and perception problems), the career practitioner decided to broach the subject of Steve's wife coming in for a session. The career practitioner stated, "Steve, it seems like we are really uncovering a lot of interesting information related to your values and interests as they relate to potential occupational options. I am curious of your thoughts about having Ally come in for our next session to discuss our results. You have talked about how it is hard to explain your situation to her as well as your desire for her to understand. Having Ally join us could help with some of your concerns. What do you think?"

Steve was at first hesitant, saying "Uh, I'm not sure. Ally and I don't really talk much about specifics of my rehab. I think it might be a little awkward."

The career practitioner acknowledged his concern and informed him how the conversation would be handled. "Steve, I understand it can be tough to discuss things that aren't pleasant. I see this as us working together to ensure we are all on the same page regarding your career decision. You have indicated your struggle in helping her understand. It might be helpful for us to have that discussion together with my providing my views of our work to this point. It could help us all work together as you determine your options moving forward."

Steve agreed, adding, "I guess it would be help-

ful for you to talk about our work. I am not that good at communicating details and get frustrated. It might be good to have you talk about it to help her understand."

After Steve and his career practitioner discussed how the conversation would transpire, Steve's wife, Ally, agreed to come in to the next session. During that session, the career practitioner shared the purpose of the meeting, the goals of Steve's work in counseling, and results of his assessments. Ally was also provided the opportunity to offer her thoughts on the situation and ask questions regarding the process. The meeting ended with an agreement to keep each other informed of progress to the degree it was appropriate and relevant to Ally and Steve. Steve and his career practitioner processed the meeting in their next individual counseling session, with Steve indicating the meeting seemed to be helpful and had improved his and his wife's communication during the week between sessions.

Given the new understanding of Steve's interests and values, the career practitioner and Steve co-constructed an integrated future developing goals and actions steps. This future involved Steve examining his mechanical repair and engineering options both in the civilian and military workforce. Since the decision of Steve's medical discharge was not determined during the current term of counseling, it was important to consider both civilian and military occupational options related to his values, interests, and skills. The career practitioner and Steve developed strategies for investigating his options, including effective decision-making strategies. Steve was also encouraged to view his situation as a developmental process. The career practitioner and Steve determined he had moved into the Synthesis phase of his CASVE cycle with a discussion related to the future steps in the process.

Steve's career counseling experience along with methods for applying the cycle in future career decisions was processed. Steve shared that he felt he had obtained a sense of control over the career decision. He felt that he left with a method for addressing the issue, which has helped him become an effective career decision maker both now and in the future. Steve was offered resources and the opportunity to return to the center if needed.

Summary

Guiding military personnel and veterans with disabilities through CIP and SBCC has the potential for instilling hope and creating a realistic future tied to values, interests, and skills. Cognitive information processing theory enables complex situations such as Steve's to be fully considered and understood by both the client and career practitioner when making a career decision. These two approaches may be used conjointly when working with military personnel and veterans with disabilities. The CIP focus on improving career decision making and problem solving coupled with SBCC's emphasis on abilities and instilling hope offers a goal oriented, problem-solving approach to address both current and future career decisions. A goal in career counseling is for military personnel and veterans with disabilities to feel empowered in creating fulfilling and meaningful lives for themselves.

References

Bagalman, E. (2011). Traumatic brain injury among veterans. *Congressional Research Service Report.* Retrieved from: http://www.nashia.org/pdf/tbi_among_veterans_may_2011.pdf

Berger, T.J. (2010). Testimony of Thomas J. Berger, executive director, Veteran's Health Council, regarding mental health &substance abuse issues facing returning veterans relating to criminal justice and alternatives to incarceration, *U.S. Sentencing Commission* May 17, 2010. Retrieved from: http://www.ussc.gov/Legislative_and_Public_Affairs/Public_Hearings_and_Meetings/20100317/Berger_testimony.pdf

Collins, R. C., & Kennedy, M. C. (2008). Serving families who have served: Providing family therapy and support in interdisciplinary polytrauma rehabilitation. *Journal of Clinical Psychology: In Session 64,* 993–1003.

Keyser-Marcus, L. A., Bricout, J. C., Wehman, P., Cambell, L. R., Cifu, D. X., Englander, J., High, W., & Zafonte, R. D. (2002). Acute predictors of return to employment after traumatic brain injury: A longitudinal follow-up. *Archives of Physical Medicine and Rehabilitation, 83,* 635–6–40.

Marchione, M. (2012, May 27). Iraq, Afghanistan veterans filing for disability benefits at historic rate. *Huffington Post.* Retrieved from http://www.huffingtonpost.com/2012/05/27/iraq-afghanistan-veterans-disability-benefits_n_1549436.html.

Office of the Deputy Under Secretary of Defense. (2005). 2005 *demographics report.* Retrieved from Purdue University, Military Family Research Institute website: http://www.acq.osd.mil/ie/ie_library_archive.shtml#rpts

Sammons, M. T., & Batten, S. V. (2008). Psychological service for returning veterans and their families: Evolving conceptualization of the sequelae of war-zone experiences. *Journal of Clinical Psychology: In Session 64,* 921–927.

Sampson, J.P. Jr., Peterson, G.W., Lenz, J.G., Reardon, R.C., & Saunders, D.E. (1996). Career Thoughts Inventory. Odessa, FL: Psychological Assessment Resources, Inc.

Sampson J.P., Reardon, R.C., Peterson, G.W., & Lenz, J.G. (2004). *Career counseling and services: A cognitive information processing approach.* Brooks/Cole: Belmont, CA.

Schutt, D.A. (2007) *A strength-based approach to career development using appreciative inquiry.* Broken Arrow, OK: National Career Development Association.

Seligman, M. E. (1999). Teaching positive psychology. *APA Monitor 30*(7).

Seligman, M. E. P., & Csikszentmihalyi, M. (2000). Positive psychology: An introduction. *American Psychologist, 55,* 5–14.

Smith, E. (2006). The strength-based counseling model. *The Counseling Psychologist 34,* 13–79.

Wehman, P., Targett, P., West, M., & Kregel, J. (2005). Productive work and employment for persons with traumatic brain injury: What have we learned after 20 years? *Journal of Head Trauma Rehabilitation, 20,* 115–127.

Chapter 5. Case Studies: Applying Career Development Strategies With Veterans

Chapters 1 through 4 provided information about veterans as well as potential strategies and resources for working with this population. A case study was presented in each of Chapters 2 - 4, but one case study cannot adequately present the variety of complex issues that a veteran might have. Thus, in this chapter, we present several case studies based on real veteran clients or students, each showing how the career practitioner (CP) proceeded. The responses and reflections are not meant to suggest that there is only one way to respond, but rather to provide the reader with an understanding of at least one way to respond. In addition, we discuss intervention options that could have been used but weren't and the rationale behind the choices we made. The cases were chosen for how closely they represented our "normal" experiences with veteran clients and students.

The Case of Peter

Peter was 21 years old when he joined the Army. He was the middle child of Polish immigrants who had arrived in New York with $5 in their pockets and three small children who only spoke Polish. After finishing high school, Peter enrolled in one of the local universities, but he was not successful in finishing his first semester of college. A few months later, Peter decided to join the Army. He had excellent scores on the ASVAB and was able to pick just about any Military Occupational Skill

(MOS). Because of Peter's high scores in math and science, the recruiters encouraged him to study engineering, which he agreed to do. Peter graduated at the top of his engineering class and was asked to stay on as an instructor. Even though this was a great honor, Peter declined the offer because he wanted to be involved with the troops. Soon after, Peter was assigned to a company, and he began having clashes with the persons in leadership positions.

As bright as Peter was, he could not follow orders or get along with the '"higher ups." For example, Peter was always showing up late, losing equipment, and ignoring direct orders. This behavior forced the Army to give Peter an Article 15 (non-judicial punishment) and at the end of his 3-year contract, the Army did not invite Peter to re-enlist. For the next year, Peter was able to get interviews but would only keep the jobs a couple of months, because he could not get along with his bosses. Peter also attempted to return to college, but again he could not complete his course because he would challenge the professors. Frustrated, and concerned that his current position might be ending soon, Peter decided to visit the "Vet Rep" at the local one-stop career center to identify his next steps. After some initial discussion about his reasons for seeking career assistance, the conversation focused to his present job.

Speaker	Conversation	Purpose/underlying emotions
CP:	Peter, tell me, are you happy with your present job?	Attending to emotions.
Veteran:	Well it's not the type of work I thought I would be doing, but it pays the bills.	
CP:	Are you happy with just paying the bills? From what you have told me, you went to engineering school and have tested very high on science and math abilities.	Clarifying values. Confronting inconsistencies.
Veteran:	No, not really – engineering school was a long time ago, and I have had many jobs in the Army and civilian life since I left.	

Speaker	Conversation	Purpose/underlying emotions
CP:	Peter, can you bring me a copy of your DD214 so we can see what kind of jobs you had in the Army and how they might translate to civilian work? It would also be helpful if you can bring me copies of your EERs (Enlisted Evaluation Reports) so we can look for themes that can shed light into why you get dissatisfied with your jobs.	Before proceeding with processing, the counselor wanted to make sure Peter brought in existing tools. This was written down on Peter's Individual Career Learning Plan (ICLP; see Chapter 3). An alternative would have been to save this request until the end of session.
Veteran:	That would be great because I seem to have a lot of difficulty adjusting to civilian life and keeping jobs and relationships.	
CP:	Say more about that why you think you have problems keeping jobs and also maintaining your relationships. You sound frustrated by your struggles with authority.	Exploring underlying beliefs, attending to feelings, identifying key problematic areas (i.e., authority).
Veteran:	Yes, I do lose my temper sometimes, but I have always been like that. I lose my jobs because I end up working for people who know less than me, and they think they can boss me around because I was in the Army. I had a boss that told me that if I was that smart "why did I go into the Army?" Yea, I get angry…I just want a fair chance.	"Yes…but" noted. CP also aware that suggestions made in session might be perceived as "bossing him around."
CP:	It seems you value fairness and that past interactions with supervisors have frustrated you due to not feeling like you were fairly treated. Perhaps it would be helpful to make an appointment with a counselor to get at the cause of your anger and to help you develop some strategies to deal with it at work?	Empathy, normalizing counseling, introducing mental health counseling and linking it to helping him be more successful at work. While the referral could have waited, the counselor wanted to plant the seed early in session.
Veteran:	Yeah, maybe. I guess I need to do something.	Deflection of suggestion with perhaps feigned agreement.
CP:	I think you're right. I can work with you to identify possible career options, but it seems like the anger has been getting in the way of your being successful. We can come back to that later. In the meantime, would you be interested in taking a career inventory? I'm thinking that maybe your interests have changed over time.	The counselor chose to strengthen Peter's statement of agreement rather than confront the possible authenticity of it, and to reinforce the link between anger and his lack of success. The counselor then chose to change course, again to let the counseling idea simmer, and to help Peter expand his options through an assessment. The CP could have continued to focus on why Peter wasn't successful but wanted him to have a tangible positive outcome of the session and to feel they were moving forward.
Veteran:	Yes, because I would like to have opportunities to have better paying jobs.	
CP:	Peter, I would think that with your ability levels we should explore more careers rather than just jobs. Was there a career that you had always thought of having?	Encouragement, slight confrontation, opening the conversation towards exploration of options.

Speaker	Conversation	Purpose/underlying emotions
Veteran:	Not really, but I have always liked working with my hands.	Realistic theme noted. Also noted that he denied that he was considering any options.
CP:	So, what were your goals when you enrolled in college the last few times?	The CP decided to back up to when he enrolled in college to have some ideas of the options he liked.
Veteran:	Actually, academics have always come easy for me, and I thought my family expected me to get a degree.	Deflection of the question, some family pressure starting to seep in.
CP:	Peter, what comes naturally to you besides academics?	Third attempt at identifying interests and options.
Veteran:	Actually, working with my hands — not just mechanics, but I draw and I am also athletic.	This seemed to work better. Counselor noted that perhaps there was a lack of information about career options.
CP:	Peter, it seems to me that you are very talented and have many career options. Have you accessed your GI Bill?	Encouragement, clarification of the resources available, helpful to know as they consider options and training requirements.
Veteran:	Yes, numerous times during my tour. I recently finished psychology and chemistry.	
CP:	How is that going for you?	Counselor provided a general question, attempting to see if interests were emerging.
Veteran:	Not well. Again. (sigh). I seem to have difficulty getting along with the instructors. Sometimes I think that I may know more about the subject than the instructor…and then I end up either dropping the class or failing.	Unexpected response. Anger issue emerging again.
CP:	So it seems like the personal and social issues are not only impacting your success at work, but also your success in school. Peter, we talked about this earlier, and you seemed hesitant. This is the second time that you've talked about how your anger is impacting your achieving your goals. How do you feel now about making an appointment with a counselor so you can discuss the social and behavioral issues you are dealing with?	Confrontation, immediacy ("you seemed hesitant"). Forthright questioning about making an appointment.
Veteran:	That sounds like a good idea. Maybe they can help me with my marital issues and I can start a new life. Can you make sure you refer me to someone who knows what they are talking about?	Other issues (i.e., marital) emerge.
CP:	Absolutely. Here is the number for the VA who can help you set up an appointment with behavioral health. I've spoken to the practitioners on many occasions and can tell you that not only are they skilled in their field, but also with issues specific to veterans. We can make the call from my office when we are done today. Meanwhile, we can start the career exploration.	Referral given and plan to make the appointment from the office. The CP decided to offer this as a way to "strike while the iron was hot," when Pete was in agreement that he needed to address the anger issues. Once a plan was made, this freed the CP to continue focusing on career exploration.

Reflection on Peter's Case

Peter would be a challenge for any career practitioner, mainly because of his high ability levels and his low social skills. Given his tendency to question the knowledge and skills of employers and instructors, it is likely that Peter might have similar feelings towards the career practitioner. In later sessions, the career practitioner would use immediacy and confrontation when sensing that Peter was pushing back on suggestions.

Notice the career practitioner asked Peter to bring in copies of his EER (Enlisted Evaluation Reports). These evaluation reports will shed some light into Peter's ability to work with others as assessed by his supervisors; they are very important in the military, being used for promotion purposes as well as continuity of service. The request to see the EER also was an important request by the career practitioner as it communicated competency to Peter. Other branches of the military have similar reports, such as the Enlisted Performance Report (EPR) for the Air Force and the Fitness Report (FITREP) for the Navy.

Peter did not finish using his GI Bill and ended up losing it, which prompted his consulting a career practitioner. Peter revealed to his career practitioner that he was on wife number four and had had more than 20 different jobs, mostly blue collar, anything that involved the outside and working with his hands. He would first succeed, but then he would get fired. The longest he had been able to maintain a job was laying cable for a long-distance telephone company, a job he found through the Vet Center. After getting the job, he stopped seeing the career practitioner on a regular basis and also stopped mental health counseling. He occasionally drops by the career practitioner's office to touch base. He has been at that phone company for five years, but continues to feel devalued as others with less experience have been promoted and he has not.

Knowing how veterans function in the military can be very helpful in possibly predicting career directions. In this case, it was best for the career practitioner to encourage Peter to seek mental health counseling while he explored other possibilities for future careers. Unfortunately for Peter, he had already lost his GI Bill and did not qualify for Vocational Rehabilitation because he did not have a service-connected disability. However, Peter can use the Vet Center for counseling and the main VA office on a space available basis. This case is an example of how mental health and career issues interact, and how a career practitioner might use tools familiar to the veteran (such as the EER form and Form DD214) to help connect the veteran with appropriate referrals and to continue with career counseling. It also shows that despite our best efforts, some clients will have difficulty implementing necessary changes.

The Case of Joe

Joe is 24 years old and considers his home to be in the Daytona Beach, Florida area. Joe graduated from high school at the age of 16 through the international baccalaureate (IB) program. Had he continued with the program, he would have completed four years of high school with an associate degree of his choice. The reasoning behind Joe leaving the program early and continuing onto a mainstream Florida public university was primarily influenced by Joe's "coming out to his parents" as a homosexual at 16 and them deciding that his life "choice" was not suitable while residing in their household. Joe then attended a local university and, for the first time in his life, he experienced failure, obtaining the first two Fs of his scholastic history. According to Joe, he was just too young to be in a university setting. After the first semester, Joe chose to make it on his own working full time while continuing towards his pre-med degree at a local community college. This went on for a few months. According to Joe, after the complete exhaustion of it all, he chose to "better himself" by "diving into the unknown" through enlisting into the Air Force (USAF).

Joe graduated from USAF Basic Training and from there became a Dental Assistant at his first duty station, Andrews Air Force Base, Maryland. Joe loved living in the Washington, DC region. He obtained his first overseas assignment less than two years later, and he was assigned to a dental flight in Europe for two years. During that time, he longed for deployments on the front line due to the excitement and quick problem solving required. In the past year, though, he began to enjoy those deployments less and less. He failed four physical training (PT) tests in a 24-month period and subsequently was discharged for "unbecoming actions to fulfill his duties as an airman in the United States Air Force." This is an honorable separation, but suggests that there were some issues with the service member, such as being overweight or underweight, having an affair, and so forth.

Part of the issue for the discharge was the emergence of new set regulations on height, weight, and waistlines, in which every newly set minimum must be met. At the time, Joe was 6'3", 240 pounds, and had a 39-inch waist, but that it is unsatisfactory now according to the USAF. While Joe could work on reducing his waist measurement by excelling on his runtime, push-ups, and sit-ups,

he continued to exceed the maximum waist size for the Air Force during his annual physical tests. Joe was very frustrated because he really wanted to comply with the body requirements of the Air Force, but there was nothing he could do about his large frame.

Joe separated from the military with an honorable discharge, and while he was not at all disappointed in himself for his achievements in the USAF, he was extremely disappointed in the organization that he trusted. Joe stated that because they randomly changed the standards, he was now being fired. Joe stated that he has become comfortable with the notion of leaving the military, and planned on using his GI Bill benefits to become a full-time student for the next three years. Joe's most pressing concerns were about choosing a major, finances, health care coverage, and housing. He made an appointment with a career practitioner at the university to help him with the decision of choosing a major.

Speaker	Conversation	Purpose/underlying emotions
CP:	Joe, you seem to have a very good grasp of your transition to civilian life.	Encouragement.
Veteran:	Yes, I recognize the reality, even though it hurts my feelings. I took the TAP course that my base offered to separating service members, and it was very helpful.	
CP:	What did you find most helpful about it?	Information gathering, seeing what was helpful in the past to help plan future interventions.
Veteran:	First of all, I met the other service members that were separating, and we agreed to stay in touch and share job opportunities as they came up. They also had the VA representatives, financial counselors, and some of the university representatives to give us information on the education bill.	Notes that support from other veterans and having specific individuals were valuable to Joe.
CP:	You mentioned that the Air Force trained you as a dental technician. Is that something that still interests you?	Acknowledging past training, exploring current interests.
Veteran:	Yes, actually I was thinking about using my GI benefits to finish my undergraduate degree and then applying to dental school. But then again, maybe I just think I want to be a dentist because I worked with them. I've actually been thinking about being a mental health counselor.	Need: exploration and/or confirmation.

Speaker	Conversation	Purpose/underlying emotions
CP:	OK. So would you like to start researching those occupations, or are you interested in learning about other occupations that might match your interests and skills?	CP indicating that Joe is able to make a good decision on how to proceed, but to avoid overwhelming him, provides two general options.
Veteran:	Could we do both?	
CP:	Of course. Let's write that down on your plan. You also mentioned that you had some concerns over finances, health coverage, and housing?	CP indicating that attention had been paid to Joe's non-career concerns.
Veteran:	Yes, I have some money saved up, and I know that I have 180 days after separation where I can continue to use my TRICARE. I also plan on visiting the VA to get my spine evaluated. If they find a disability, I can then enroll in Vocational Rehabilitation.	
CP:	It sounds like you've thought through what you need to do next.	CP decided not to focus on disability but to emphasize the positive steps Joe had taken in making a decision. CP may refer back to this decision as they discuss how Joe would like to address the career concern.
Veteran:	Yes, I hope everything goes my way this time because you know I had problems the first time I went to college.	Some fatalistic, external wishing noticed.
CP:	Yes, you shared that was the first time you had ever received Fs.	
Veteran:	Yeah, I am usually an excellent student. I don't really know what happened with me. I think I became depressed and I may not be out of it yet.	Client raising concerns of the impact of depression on his current situation.
CP:	Are you seeing someone at the VA for your depression and unresolved issues from your youth?	Rather than assess the depression, the CP accepts Joe's terminology and asks about counseling. CP chose to do this because of the unresolved issues with parents. Another option would have been for the CP to have administered a Career Thoughts Inventory to determine the degree and nature of negative career thoughts.
Veteran:	Yes, I just started seeing someone.	
CP:	Good, I'm glad to see you're getting some help. OK. Let's focus on helping you decide on a major. We can start by looking at typical majors that dentists and counselors choose. If you'd like, you could bring in any information you have on your skills, military experience, and so on, and we can see if there are other options that might jump out of us.	Purpose for career service becoming clearer. CP mentally notes that collaboration with Joe's counselor might be necessary, especially if both are addressing negative thinking. CP also demonstrates knowledge of and value for Joe's experiences.
Veteran:	Sure thing. That sounds like a good plan.	

Reflection on Joe's Case

Joe returned to the career practitioner the following week. Based on the career practitioner's recommendations, he had used the O*NET military crosswalk to generate civilian options similar to his work in the USAF. While the majority of occupations listed were dental (e.g., dentist, hygienist, dental laboratory technician, prosthodontics), Joe stated that he clicked on "related occupations" and came up with a few of interest, specifically, respiratory therapist, optometrist, and physical therapist. The career practitioner and Joe went over the pages he had printed out and noted similarities among the fields in terms of interests, values, and education. Joe decided that because the majority of his career interest was in the medical field, he would focus on a pre-med major.

The career practitioner regularly checked in with Joe about his feelings related to his situation and his progress in career counseling. The career practitioner administered the Career Thoughts Inventory to identify the nature of the negative thinking, which resulted in very high overall scores, as well as high scores on all three subscales. They often used cognitive reframing when the negative statements seemed to slow down the process. For example, when Joe first identified the related occupations, the career practitioner asked him to read the job descriptions and "give voice" to whatever was going on in his mind as he read, i.e. his self-talk. This revealed many negative beliefs, such as "Who am I kidding, I'm not smart enough," or "What makes me think I'd even be accepted?"

Joe was another example of a very bright and capable veteran having problems with his integration from military to civilian life. In Joe's case, he seemed to have a good plan, and came across as being stable and high functioning. However, Joe had many unresolved issues from his youth. He continued to work with his career practitioner and engaged in mental health counseling simultaneously. With Joe's permission, the career practitioner and the counselor spoke on several occasions about strategies that seemed to be working with respect to his negative self-talk.

An important point is that of Joe's discharge for "unbecoming actions to fulfill his duties as an airman in the United States Air Force." In Joe's case, it is still considered an honorable discharge, which is an important aspect when applying for jobs in the civilian sector. Helping Joe learn how to answer questions about why he left the military in a way that is positive will be important for successful interviewing. Possible responses to that question might include "It was just time for something different," or "I have many different goals for myself. I wanted to serve my country, which is why I joined the military. That phase of my life will always be special. However, now I want to focus on using my skills and education in a different setting." Joe had many career and personal issues to address, necessitating many sessions with the career practitioner. By creating a plan, the career practitioner was able to relieve the sense of being overwhelmed by co-creating manageable goals and sequencing activities in a way that decreased stress and increased hope.

The Case of Tom

Tom came from a long line of military members, which included his grandfather, father, mother, and older brother. Tom joined the Army when he was 23 years old after graduating from college. Even though he had a college degree in criminal justice and qualified to be an officer, he wanted to be where the action was. Tom decided to join right away even though his new wife was against it. "Military is just who I am," he would say. He went off to basic training and then off to school to be a combat engineer. Right after graduating from engineering school, he received his orders to deploy along with the news that he was going to be a father of twins. Tom was very excited about his orders and the news of his twins. He had mixed feelings about leaving his wife behind pregnant with twins, but this is what the military expected from him. He remembered that old military saying "if we wanted you to have children, we would have issued you some."

Tom spent the first week of his deployment being transported to a Forward Operating Base

(FOB) in Iraq. His first few days there were hot, and he thought he was going to melt. He told his wife that he had sand everywhere and that it was almost impossible to see when the sand began to blow. For the first few weeks, Tom was very bored and wished he would get to see some action. He would entertain himself writing letter to his wife and unborn babies. Finally, his opportunity came up when the first sergeant asked for volunteers to drive a convoy to the next FOB. Tom jumped at the opportunity. An hour down the road, Tom remembers thinking that this convoy was not too bad of a job, and he wouldn't mind doing it a couple of more times. This was the last thing Tom remembers from that day. What Tom didn't remember was that the truck he was in hit an Improvised Explosive Devise (IED), and he was the only survivor of six soldiers. He was immediately evacuated to Germany where he spent two months before he was transferred to Walter Reed Hospital. Tom suffered burns over 40% of his body, lost eyesight in both his eyes, and lost the use of his legs. Tom is 25 years old now, 100% disabled, and lives with his 23-year old wife and one-year old twin boys at his parents' home. Tom recognized that he was permanently injured, but he believed that he still had a lot to offer his family. He wanted to continue working in his college degree and preferably with other veterans. This is why he sought career counseling.

Speaker	Conversation	Purpose/underlying emotions
CP:	Tom, according to your records you have a degree and training as an engineer form the Army. I also note from your DD214 that you had some OJT (on the job training) as an instructor while at engineering school.	CP chose to start with Tom's strengths and accomplishments rather than the disability.
Veteran:	Yes, and I really liked teaching the other soldiers. It's just, since I got wounded…	Tom speaks positively about those skills and interests, but quickly focuses on his disability. Counselor also considers PTSD as a possibility.
CP:	How are you doing with your injuries?	Attentiveness to client main concern.
Veteran:	It's been almost two years since my accident. I live with my wife and my parents, but I need to get back to working.	CP considers whether shame and guilt are present.
CP:	What kind of work would you like to do?	CP could have focused more on feelings associated with previous statement, but as client seems focused on negatives, wanted to help the client start to shift more to the future, using positive words.
Veteran:	I really liked engineering school…I think I can still work with engineering…Maybe I can still teach.	Less negativity showing.
CP:	Well, let's look at what vocational rehabilitation has to offer. [He had been recuperating at a hospital, but he had not been to vocational rehabilitation yet. It is also typical that nothing else would be started until the veteran is medically cleared]. Because you are classified as being 100% disabled, you quality for rehabilitation and free schooling. We need to also check into the VA program that pays a stipend to family members that are full-time caretakers of their injured veteran.	CP could have spent more time exploring initial options, but instead chose to share information already known to the CP (i.e., that Tom would qualify) and to provide encouraging news and instill hope.

Speaker	Conversation	Purpose/underlying emotions
Veteran:	That would be great. My wife and family have been taking care of me full time. I'm tired of just sitting around. I need to be doing something. I may not look like much, but I'm a pretty smart guy. There must be some work out there that I can do.	CP notices additional shame and guilt.
CP:	I'm sure there is. Have you done any research into possible positions?	CP could address the shame and guilt, but given that this was a first session, chose instead to redirect the client to the positive steps that have already been or that could be taken.

Reflection on Tom's Case

Tom's career interest in engineering didn't end with the occurrence of his disability. He seemed to have a mostly positive attitude about his ability to work, albeit many negative feelings about how he is currently not working. He did not seem to be struggling with negative cognitions about employment, although the negative feelings about his current situation were very evident. When asked about these in a future session, Tom acknowledged that he hated being dependent on others and that a great deal of his identity was wrapped up in being active.

At one point, Tom said, "I'm just a slug, a good-for-nothing, disgusting slug. I'm barely moving." This metaphor revealed concerns about how his wife and in-laws saw him, which in turn gave way to feelings of intense self-loathing. After several minutes of allowing Tom to feel and describe that image, the career practitioner asked Tom to create a metaphor to represent what he would like to be in six months. Tom thought about it and said, "The Jolly Green Giant." He went on to explain that he wanted to be happy, larger than life, able to do whatever he wanted to do, overcome all obstacles, and teach others to do the same. The career practitioner asked Tom if he could recapture the image of the slug, and then picture the transformation from slug to giant. They then discussed what that transformation was like visually, and began to speak about what practically would need to take place in order for Tom to see evidence of the transformation. Other projective tools such as the Decision Space Worksheet or early memories might

have yielded similar responses, but because Tom had introduced a metaphor, the career practitioner chose to stay with that intervention.

The career practitioner also connected Tom with the Vet Success Program for job training, job search support, and apprenticeships. As part of their discussions, the career practitioner assessed Tom's knowledge of accommodations that he would need to perform the work, of which he was very well aware, and worked on networking strategies to locate teaching opportunities.

The Case of Pam

The Yellow Ribbon program was designed to help the Guard and Reserves reintegrate back to civilian life. This program is usually during the weekend with many presenters speaking on topics ranging from mental health to financial planning. All service members are encouraged to bring their families. During this two day event, the units pay for babysitting while the parents spend time in the sessions.

Pam was a post-deployment member of a Yellow Ribbon Women's weekend group. She shared that she had always wanted to be in the military, but her parents insisted she go to college first. She graduated with a degree in communications and had a hard time getting a job. She decided this was the time to fulfill her dreams and began visiting recruiters. Because Pam had a degree, she qualified to become an officer. However, at that time, there were no available military schools for her, so she decided she would join the National Guard of her state and continue to look for a job. This was one week before 9/11. Pam recalled how quickly her phone rang on that date, and that she was activated immediately. Since her initial activation, Pam had been deployed four times, two of these for more than one year at a time in different FOBs. Pam's dream of being in the military came partly true, but there were consequences to her active duty. As a member of the Yellow Ribbon Women's group, one weekend she shared that because she had so many activations, she had not had an opportunity to look for a civilian job. Pam felt that no one would hire her with a degree that was 10 years old and with no experience in what she studied. Pam had worked as a public affairs officer in Iraq and Afghanistan as well as in her National Guard wing.

As Pam shared her experiences, she became quiet and melancholy. The other women asked her what was triggering this reaction. She indicated she was struggling with memories of her deployments. When this question was asked, four of the other women who had also been deployed with Pam looked at each other. The career practitioner (CP) running the group, who was also a veteran, reminded Pam and the group that this was a safe place to share some of their troubling experiences. Pam began to tear up and began screaming that she had enough of being harassed and threatened. The other women seemed to know exactly what Pam was talking about. The CP had a feeling of what might have happened to Pam, and possibly the women downrange, and decided to disclose some of her (the therapist's) Military Sexual Trauma (MST) experienced during her time in the Army. The other four women immediately opened up and shared their experiences. Then Pam related her experience.

Pam spoke about being sent to a FOB where there were no women. When she arrived, the cadre was not aware of her assignment, so they did not know where to put her or what to do with her. Pam had no problems being the only woman in the camp or having to sleep in a separate tent. However, she did have a problem with some of the local military who were allowed to use the base. She shared that numerous times when she was taking a shower in an impromptu stall with just a piece of board on one side, she would find either the locals or the junior service members staring or looking at her. Similar behaviors would occur when she needed to use the bathroom, which was out of hearing or eye range of the tents. On numerous occasions, her towel would be missing so when she finished her shower, she could not cover herself. Twice, she was followed to her tent and watched through the seams as she dressed.

Pam's frustration and sense of helplessness was due to her inability to report these acts. She was told right up front that they "did not want a whining" or complaining female in their FOB. This created a huge dilemma for Pam who just wanted to do her job like anyone else. The other four women in the group agreed that similar things happened to them in another FOB. For Pam, her struggles with unwanted sexual harassment changed when a group of Marines arrived at FOB. Pam had decided to reduce her intake of liquids as to minimize her bathroom trips and avoid the sexual harassment she endured whenever she had to pull down her pants. She quickly became dehydrated and passed out.

When she was interviewed by the medic as to why she was dehydrated, she was initially berated, being reminded that she was a seasoned military member (and should know better). At that point, she shared her story. When the small contingency of Marines found out what had been happening to the female captain, they immediately took over. She was escorted to showers and a latrine with a Marine standing nearby, and her tent was moved near the Marine tent. The Marines had a very "pointed" talk with the men that took part in the harassment and suggested that they may want to stop it immediately. Pam was very grateful to the Marines and the harassment stopped immediately with no backlash. Still, the experiences haunted Pam to this day.

Future group sessions focused more on current life issues, which for Pam, was deciding what to do next for her career. While the group checked in on her each week about her progress on her decision, she decided to work with the career practitioner on an individual basis.

Reflection on Pam's Case

The main purpose of this Yellow Ribbon Women's group was to provide support for the women that had just returned from deployment. The career practitioner group leader was a woman veteran who understood the frustration the women experienced downrange. The group was encouraged to share some of their experiences during deployment. This particular session was very cathartic for Pam and the other female members. MST is a serious trauma, as described in Chapter 1. The decision to self-disclose is always an ethical one. The career practitioner needed to be sure that the intention behind the self-disclosure was for Pam's good, not for her own relief. Because of Pam's intense reaction, coupled with the unwillingness of Pam and the other women in the group to state the obvious, the career practitioner decided it would be in everyone's best interest to open the discussion on MST. By the career practitioner's sharing of her experience with MST, it helped the other women share about their experiences. They no longer felt alone in their experiences, anger, or fear.

The future sessions allowed Pam to focus on her career issues. Even though Pam had a continuing job to return to as a playback technician, she was considering looking for another career. Pam had been working in a radio station when she got activated and sent downrange. During her deployment she worked as a Communication Specialist in the area of intelligence. This communication specialist position in the military was a job Pam really enjoyed, however, she was having trouble locating similar work in the civilian arena. By working with the career practitioner, Pam recognized that she had options on what career she wanted to follow. She had always thought that she was pretty much "stuck" as a playback technician, but she was able to reframe that as one of many options that would provide her an income while returning to college to expand her education in the area of intelligence.

The Case of Angela

Angela served as a nurse in the Army. She enlisted right out of high school and obtained her degree in nursing during her time in the military. Angela is a second-generation immigrant from a family that highly valued education. Angela married her high-school sweetheart, who was also in the military. They have three grown children.

Angela was moving along with her career. She was being continually promoted related to her positive performance reviews. Angela had become a surgery nurse and valued the sense of importance in the work as well as status this position offered. Rapidly ascending through the ranks, she completed her master's degree in nursing. She had begun to feel the military would be a long-term career for her. After serving for 20 years in the military, her husband decided to retire, leaving Angela as the only one working in their marriage.

Angela had suffered a moderate traumatic brain injury related to a mortar explosion during her deployment to a military hospital in Afghanistan. She had suffered deficits in her memory, making it difficult for her to remember orders in the highly active and stressful environment of an operating room. This new reality had created questions for Angela related to her career in the military. Her apparent inability to function to the degree she was able to prior to the injury created stress and anxiety related to her career options moving forward. Her plan to make the military a life-long career was now in question. This uncertainty created tension in her marriage as her memory issues affected her ability to complete simple household tasks. Angela came to a university career center that had established a relationship with the local VA clinic to provide career counseling to military personnel and veterans in need.

Speaker	Conversation	Purpose/underlying emotions
CP:	Angela, you shared a little of your struggle with feeling like you were on a specific path in the Army as a surgery nurse that may or may not be available to you. How is that for you?	Paraphrase, asking deeper questions, checking in with emotions.
Veteran:	It's really tough. I felt like things were moving along in a certain direction in the Army and then this happened. It is hard to understand how this happened.	
CP:	You also seemed to enjoy your work and the degree you were helping people in a tangible way. You have mentioned how education is important to you and you were using your education to advance your career. Now you sense that your injury is limiting you.	Acknowledging feelings, linking values and interests to loss, empathizing.
Veteran:	I am just not sure what I can do now. I have considered options, but I did not work hard in school to work in jobs that don't require an education. The reason I am unsure of what to do is tied to my not feeling I can function the way I used to as a surgery nurse.	CP notes that Angela sees the connection between being stuck and thoughts/emotions.
CP:	Angela, I am wondering about your options. Obviously, the injury has been difficult for you, making things uncertain for you. You seem to value helping people and working in a position that uses your education. I wonder about exploring options that offer opportunities aligned with these values to determine potential opportunities going forward.	Acknowledging pain, focusing on increasing options. The counselor could also have reinforced the link between negative thoughts and feeling stuck, or asked Angela to describe the options she had considered in the past.
Veteran:	That makes sense. I do like the potential to continue to work and hope to do something of importance that requires an education. While I am not young, I still have quite a few years to work. I would like to work and contribute in some way.	
CP:	That makes sense. I am thinking we can complete a Self-Directed Search that explores interests and assesses occupations that align with these interests. We will talk through the assessment together to ensure you can ask any questions if needed. What do you think?	Linking goal of expanding options to specific inventory. Outlines a short-term plan, asks for client input. Another option would be to assess for negative thinking first.

Speaker	Conversation	Purpose/underlying emotions
Veteran:	That makes sense. As long as I can touch base with you during the test, I think I will do all right.	
CP:	Yes, I will be right here. Remember, there is no right or wrong answer to the inventory. You can't fail it. One thing I would like for us to consider is how this process is for you. You have indicated your current situation has been stressful and has affected your relationship with your husband. I hope you feel you can talk about the stress associated with this career decision and how it is affecting you as well as your relationship with your husband.	CP addresses the issue of test performance as well as related stress. CP opens the door for discussing the impact of anxiety on herself and her husband.
Veteran:	I appreciate that. It has been hard both for me and my husband. While our focus is on my career issues, it does help to be able to talk about how this is for me to deal with this situation.	

Reflections on Angela's Case

Angela was not only dealing with a career decision, but also the sense of loss over potentially losing her career that offered a sense of importance and status in her position as a surgery nurse. The career practitioner certainly considered the career challenges she is facing, but it is important to consider all aspects of her experience. She is somewhat grieving the loss of her identity. Her education, which was significantly important to her and within her family, was at risk of being irrelevant to her career development. The career practitioner's introduction of the Self-Directed Search was designed to offer hope and align alternative options that still align with her interests and skills if she is in fact unable to work as surgery nurse. This would fit into the Synthesis-Elaboration Process described in Chapter 3. The work going forward will involve the career practitioner discussing her functionality, exploring her options going forward, and focusing on her career-decision making process, and monitoring stress and anxiety associated with her career development. Other options would be to use the Occupations Finder (Holland) to identify options with the same code as surgical nurse, or to use O*NET to explore careers related to surgical nursing. Should negative thinking continue to come up in the conversation, the career practitioner might administer the Career Thoughts Inventory (Sampson et al., 1996).

The Case of Greg

Greg, a male in his late 20s, had enlisted in the Air Force and had spent 6 years there. He was not disabled, but had separated from the military to pursue a college degree and a career in sports broadcasting. He had enrolled in a university career course designed specifically for veterans. Greg was disruptive, disrespectful, and noncompliant during the first several weeks of the course. He avoided the instructor and graduate assistant, and made it known to the instructor he would only complete assignments he saw value in. Greg verbalized that he already knew most of this information and took the course not to learn all of this kiddy stuff but to get direct leads in the field he wanted to pursue — sports broadcasting. He was confident he was better qualified for these "civilian" jobs than any of the "civilians" he would have to compete with because of his military experience. He had obtained two internships in broadcasting, but they did not work out and were ended early. However, he still believed he would be hired with his degree in the field of broadcasting once he finished his education.

Greg refused three invitations from the instructor for a meeting to discuss his classroom behavior and academic performance. His behavior was clearly in violation of the student code of conduct and would require a referral to the Dean of Students if it didn't change. To avoid having to make a referral, the instructor spoke to the Director of Veteran Services about Greg. Greg had worked for a brief time for the director, and the instructor hoped that the director might be able to get through to Greg. The student did meet with the Director of the Veteran Services Office who reviewed Greg's conduct in the classroom and warned him of possible consequences. Greg continued to avoid the instructor, but his in-class behavior was appropriate after meeting with the director.

Greg graduated in the spring 2010. That fall, he signed up for the Career Center's alumni services. He reported having difficulty getting a job. When asked about his plan to go into sports broadcasting, he reported that he had given that up. Greg was intent on believing that his résumé was the key to his job search. He wrote and rewrote many résumés. He was getting selected for interviews with name brand companies, which typically means the résumé is working just fine and doing its job — getting interviews. He reported he was typically rejected. Greg would usually get rejected after he would tell the interviewer how he would do things if he employed in that company. He resented being interviewed for "entry level" positions.

Reflection on Greg's Case

This is a good example of a veteran student who just did not understand the civilian process or expectations for employment. He rejected the opportunity he had in the Veteran Success course to obtain accurate and realistic information about professional level employment. He was stuck on

the formula of a good resume = getting a job. While he was respectful with the instructor after meeting with the director, for the remainder of the course, he did the bare minimum on assignments. Following graduation, nothing much had changed. Greg continued to fail to impress interviewers. With the frustration of being rejected by employers, Greg eventually became receptive to feedback in regards to the job search process. As an alumnus, he began meeting with a career practitioner and, in future sessions, negative career thoughts were addressed with cognitive restructuring. In subsequent sessions, he demonstrated his understanding and ability to reframe his negative career thoughts. Even though Greg was unreceptive to the information shared in the career course, the course may have planted the seed about what career services were available to him and, when he was ready, he returned and began to benefit from them.

Summary

The cases presented in this chapter were based on real cases drawn from the experiences of the authors. Career counseling with veterans may require inquiry into other issues and needs, such as military sexual trauma, basic living skills, and homelessness. The purpose of this chapter was to show that veterans have experiences which can complicate the career-decision making process, but they also have career concerns that are similar to other clients. Career practitioners can use common techniques and tools to help veterans progress through the career decision-making process, but they may need to be aware of resources specific to veterans, which were highlighted in this chapter and throughout this book.

Chapter 6. Teaching an Undergraduate Career Class for Veterans

Creating a veteran-friendly atmosphere has become a priority on many college campuses. As veterans begin their transition from military to student life, many are unsure of which major to pursue. Some will want to find a major and a career similar to the work that they did in the military, while others will want to explore completely different options. While several options exist for addressing these needs, we wanted to describe how one university went about accomplishing this goal through the creation and delivery of an undergraduate career-planning course specific to veterans. In this chapter, we describe how the course was developed, designed, and evaluated, followed by a reflection and recommendations for future courses.

Case Presentation

John was an Army veteran. He had spent three years on active duty, then separated to use his education benefits to attend college. John did not attend college prior to enlisting in the Army and, while on active duty he was not stationed close enough to a college to attend classes. He took a few general education courses at one of his assignments on an Army post. In addition, he knew his technical training in the Army was worth some college credit.

John was unsure of the career he wanted to pursue after leaving the Army, but he knew that he did not want to do what he had done in the Army, which was related to electronic communications. He also knew he did not want to be an hourly employee. He wanted to get a college degree and become a working professional, but he wasn't sure how to achieve those goals. He needed to figure out what he wanted to do and how he could find a job once he graduated. He had never looked for a job before because he enlisted right after high school.

John visited the college career center and was presented with several options: brief-assisted help where he could walk in on an as-needed basis, individual sessions with a career practitioner, group counseling focused on choosing a major, or a new career class designed especially for veterans. He chose the latter. Fortunately for John, a career course specific for veterans was being offered that semester — but the development of that course didn't happen overnight.

Establishing a Need for a Career Course for Veterans

Two years prior to John's enrolling in the course, in the fall of 2008, the Dean of Undergraduate Studies formed a Veteran Student Committee at the University of South Florida (USF) to evaluate the current capability and delivery of veteran services to the veteran student population. The committee reviewed services, processes, and support offered by other universities around the country. Over the next two years, a Veterans Support Club surveyed veterans to determine their needs and, in response, the Dean of Undergraduate Studies created a committee to develop a career course specific to veterans.

The purpose of the undergraduate elective course for new veteran students was to help them transition into college life and prepare for their transition from university life to civilian work life. The committee had representation from the Veterans Services Office, the Dean of Undergraduate Studies, the Counseling Center, the Career Center, and the Transitional Advising Office (TRAC) that also manages the university experience course. A number of the committee members were veterans who were able to provide the committee first-hand testimony about their transitions from military life to civilian/student life at the University of South Florida. This included veterans who had separated from the military short of retirement, some who had separated because of a disability, and some who had retired from the military and transitioned into second careers.

The committee had many discussions to shape the goals of the course. Reardon, Folsom, Lee, and Clark (2011) identified three types of career courses offered in four-year colleges: those with an emphasis on career-decision making, those concentrating on job search preparation, and specialized courses geared toward a specific discipline. The committee decided to focus this course on job search preparation to assist veterans with the transition from the military to the university and from the university to the world of work.

Veterans Success Course: Two Components

The course was designed with two components and was an adaptation of the university experience class offered to freshmen students during their first semester at USF. The first component included content on adjusting to the college campus. The equivalent of one-credit hour of material to help our veteran students adjust to college life was taught during the first five weeks of the 15-week course. The Director of Veterans Services selected two veterans to teach this part of the course as adjunct instructors. Students were introduced to many student life departments and programs available to them on campus. Speakers from various departments on campus were brought in to educate the veteran students about their services and programs. In addition, the Veteran Services Office provided information about their educational benefits and brought in speakers from the VA to talk about available benefits.

The second component was an adaptation of a career-development process course offered as an elective to a variety of students at USF. Cognitive restructuring of negative career thoughts as described in Chapter 2 was included purposely. (I, Dan Van Hoose, had been one of the instructors who taught an undergraduate career course included in a study conducted by Osborn, Howard, and Leierer [2007] which demonstrated that a significant decrease in negative career thoughts could be accomplished in a short six-week career course. Seeing firsthand the benefits of addressing negative career thoughts in my other career classes, I purposely wanted to include this topic in this course).

Course Design Considerations

The committee had concerns about veteran students adjusting to an actual "brick and mortar" college campus. Many of them had probably taken courses online or attended evening classes on military installations at an education center, but most of them would not have attended traditional college campuses. Another new experience would be attending college with students who had not been in the military. Many civilian students ask questions of veteran students that the veteran students may not want to talk about. Another possible issue for veterans would be navigating the campus because USF is an extremely large urban campus with more than 40,000 students. In addition, the campus is spread over 17,000 acres, and parking can be up to a mile away from classrooms.

There was also concern about the veteran students adapting to the academic rigor of a research university. While this course was not designed to be academically difficult, it would require students to prepare for class by completing regular homework assignments. They would need to read the material in advance and be prepared to discuss the material in class. Class time was to be used to apply and implement the material students prepared for before class.

Many military training courses focus on covering material in class, and there is less emphasis on advanced preparation. For this career course, the students were expected to do quality work on their assignments and invest a reasonable amount of time doing the assignments thoroughly. In fact, this course was designed for students to spend twice as much time outside of class as in class, completing assignments. The course also required some reflective thought and insight related to students' motivations, goals, and plans for the future. In addition, military training usually focuses more on procedure and structure than on abstract thought processes. There was hope that the military experiences our veteran students had would bring them to the university with a higher level of life skills and maturity, and they would quickly adapt to the academic rigor of the university.

Development of a Course Syllabus

In this section, we review the main points and rationale behind the syllabus that was used for the course. Specifically, we address the course description, objectives, management of class time, and major assignments. The syllabus is included in Appendix D.

Course Description

The 3-credit, discussion-based, and experiential elective course was designed to facilitate a successful transition to university expectations and campus life as well as develop knowledge and skills for entering civilian employment. Overall concepts investigated included exploring campus resources, identity development, personal accountability, civic engagement, academic skills, career exploration, and job search skills. The course sought to assist military veteran students toward self-actualization and integration into the life of the campus community and prepare them for the transition from academic life to civilian employment.

Course Objectives

Six key objectives were identified for the course (See Appendix D). Many of the objectives contained specific outcomes that were similar to the objectives of the general career planning course and would be a typical objective for any career course. For this veterans' career course, we did not customize these objectives as we felt that they were useful in their original design. Thus, we used exercises and activities about the World-of Work map, a values auction, and O*NET Online to explore careers and possible majors. Others were designed considering the unique backgrounds and needs of veterans, such as objective 5. When presenting that lecture, we did not only focus on generic job search strategies, but on topics of interest to the veterans as well as resources that were veteran specific.

Course Instructors

Two career practitioners and two graduate students were selected to teach the two sections of this course. One was a retired Air Force Senior Master Sergeant and First Sergeant, who entered the Air Force with just a few college credits completed. While on active duty, he was determined to complete a degree before retiring to return to the civilian world of work. As a junior NCO, he finished an Associate of Arts degree, and added a bachelor's degree to qualifications for senior NCO, which was almost a necessity in the Air Force Recruiting Service. As a First Sergeant, he was a strong advocate for airman and NCOs in his unit continuing their education to better prepare for civilian life and promotion portfolios. He had taught the career development course numerous times beginning in 2003 for incoming freshman and for undecided/undeclared students.

The other career practitioner was from a family of veterans, and she was very interested in veterans successfully transitioning from active duty to the civilian world of work. She had done a lot of work on the Career Center website to make it veteran friendly and provide specific information for the veteran student population. She had taught the career development course several times and also participated in and was instrumental in developing the curriculum used for that course.

The two graduate assistants (GAs) were from the counselor education program in our university. One GA was assigned to each of the two sections of the Career Course. One of the graduate students had a number of veterans in her family and was quite interested in working with the veteran students. The other graduate student was also very invested in this class. Her husband was actually deployed during the semester she was assisting with this class. Needless to say, she had a lot of insight and understanding she shared with the veteran students.

This mix of backgrounds and experiences with veterans was beneficial in teaching this course, created a rich environment for the students, and helped us stay very focused on why we were teaching this course. All four of us were committed to doing our very best to help prepare these veteran students for their next transition.

Management of Class Time

Class time was organized to incorporate the active learning strategy of small groups (Osborn, 2008). The first 10 minutes of class time was used to answer any questions from the previous class meeting or about the current readings for the course. This was followed by a lecture of approximately 20–30 minutes to deliver the information and explanation necessary for acquiring knowledge and comprehension. The class (one section had 15 students, the other had 12) was then divided into small groups to discuss and process the information from the lecture. In each section, we divided the class up into two smaller groups with the instructor facilitating one of the groups and the graduate assistant facilitating the other small group. The small group time was used to process the content of the class lecture and begin work on the homework assigned for the next class meeting.

The small group discussions, processing, and homework activities lasted from 30 to 40 minutes. The class would then reconvene, and each of the groups would have an opportunity to share with the larger class what they had learned during the small group time. For example, when we covered career objectives, there were some lively discussions about the merit of having a career objective and the benefit of not having one at all. This was one of the more passionate discussions, and the input from the veteran students was most interesting. If the assignment was to write a career objective, the small group was provided a template for writing a career objective and then encouraged to complete as much of the template as possible before leaving the class.

The instructors and graduate students met weekly to review what had been done the previous week, how the classes had gone that week, what went well, and what could we do differently another time. We planned the next week's class meeting and what would be covered. We also discussed making adjustments in our teaching techniques if we thought those would be beneficial for that class topic.

Major Assignments

Assignments for this course were purposefully selected to employ active learning strategies and require higher-order thinking (Osborn, 2008). Assignments were created to include multiple-level educational objectives as defined in Bloom's (1956) taxonomy of learning. According to Bloom, there are six levels within the cognitive domain, including Knowledge (Level 1), Comprehension (Level 2), Application (Level 3), Analysis (Level 4), Synthesis (Level 5), and Evaluation (Level 6). Levels 3–6 require higher ordered thinking in that they move beyond the simple recall of information. Some of the assignments such as assigned readings, class lectures, and discussions could be classified as addressing the lower levels (Levels 1 and 2). However, most of the major assignments for the course required the educational objective of application (Level 3). The Job Search Notebook assignment required the educational objective of synthesis of the course material and content, which would be considered a Level 5 on Bloom's taxonomy.

There were two underlying goals involved in the major assignments for this course. One was the acquisition of knowledge and information, delivered through traditional lecture methods. This led to the second component, which required the student to implement and demonstrate the knowledge and information they had acquired through accomplishing a career-related task. This was achieved through the active learning strategy of the class being divided into small groups (Osborn, 2008). For example, to increase knowledge of self, the students completed self-assessments and acquired knowledge and information about the skills they possess. Including those skills in the résumé as validation of accomplishments demonstrates the ability of the student to implement that knowledge and information into their job search campaign.

Most major assignments required students to demonstrate and implement the information and knowledge they had acquired in the course. Much of this "connecting of the dots" was done in the small groups during the second half of the class meetings. Often it was one student pointing out to another student how the skills discussed in the small group were applicable to the student's résumé. In this way, the students were helping each other connect the dots and learn how to apply information and knowledge acquired in the course. The course was designed to have veteran students create the shell of a job search campaign that could be launched upon graduation.

The major assignments were selected to teach job search skills in the order used in job searching. Less time was invested in conducting self-assessment and knowledge of self because a significant amount of time was spent on these topics during the first part of the course.

Course Description and Evaluation

Several factors were considered in evaluating the Veterans Success Course. These included the degree to which the objectives were met, engagement in the class discussions, quality of work on assignments, course evaluations, comparison to sections of other career courses taught by the instructor, and the instructors' weekly reflections.

Meeting Course Objectives

The course was designed to focus on the six specific objectives, with lectures, discussion topics and assignments addressing each of these. Objectives 1–3 were the main focus of the first five weeks of this course that was taught by instructors who were skilled in the university experience course. There certainly was evidence that these objectives were met with those students who excelled in the course. For those students who did not excel in the course, the instructors' assessment was they would have been better served by focusing either on University Experience course content exclusively or focusing exclusively on Career Development.

Objectives 4, 5, and 6 had similar results. Those students who were more engaged (and typically closer to graduation) demonstrated they had attained these objectives. The evidence was in the final assignment of creating a Job Search Notebook that could be used as a shell to put together a job search campaign upon graduation. About two-thirds of the class prepared excellent notebooks, divided into sections, with their assignments from class included as guidelines and samples of how to put together a job search campaign for the transition from university life to the world of work.

Engagement in Class Discussions

The discussion about résumés and career objectives was very passionate. The class was pretty well split on the inclusion or exclusion of a career objective from their resume. A lot of their discussion about this topic was well founded. The need to get an employer's attention quickly by having a targeted, well-focused objective took some time to be appreciated. It seemed that the students kept looking at the hiring process from their perspective instead of the perspective of the employer. We used a hypothetical exercise of one of the students owning a company, and then asked that student to interview two or three other students to work in the company with the clear understanding that they would be paying their new hires out of the profit the company was making. Suddenly, the student who hypothetically owned the company became very picky about the career objective and why the other students wanted to work there. The rest of the class "got it," too.

Another animated discussion was about interviewing and how to dress for an interview. Preparing students to be new college graduates entering the world of professional level employment and interviewing for that new role included a discussion of the need to wear traditional business attire —a suit! Immediately, a number of students wanted to debate that wearing traditional business attire did not allow them to "stand out." They would look just like the rest of the candidates. They had "heard" that you needed to stand out and separate yourself. To illustrate the benefit of looking traditional and wearing traditional business clothing to the interview, we looked at some websites which had pictures of career fairs. In a number of these pictures students were dressed in traditional business attire, and they fit in well at the career fair. Inevitably, there were some students who "stood out," and the class recognized quickly that those who "stood out" did not present a favorable impression and would be more likely to be rejected.

Another topic that generated a great deal of discussion was myths and realities. Veteran students in the course frequently expressed beliefs that their previous military experience was going to make them more attractive to employers. Many of them also believed they could get paid more money to do the same thing in civilian life that they had been paid to do while on active duty. Another myth was the value of having a security clearance and how attractive that would make them to civilian employers. The difficulty of obtaining a civilian job, the competition for jobs, and the expectations civilian employers have of college graduates were clearly underestimated by veteran students.

The textbook for the course, *Military Transition to Civilian Success* (Hay, Rorrer, Rivera, Krannich, & Krannich, 2006), discussed "40 Myths and Realities" relevant to transitioning veterans. In addition, we discussed the myths and realities of transitioning veterans, such as "The clueless guy who got out of the military and somehow landed a six-figure job and a corner office with a view on his first interview" (Farley, 2010). Many of the students in this class relayed examples such as this in class. When pressed for who the people were that actually had gotten these "dream jobs," it would come out as "Well you know, I talked to this guy, who knew a guy who told him…". Students had ongoing discussions about examples given in class to sort out whether the examples were myth or reality.

Quality of Work on Class Assignments

The quality of work produced by these students was typical of other career development classes taught at the university. Some of them missed class and did not inform the instructor in advance, while others did not complete assignments on time. Those who were most motivated, who produced very high quality work, were those nearing graduation.

In designing this course, a conscious decision was made to not give quizzes to test that reading assignments had been done and that the students were preparing in advance for class. We assumed these were adult learners and would certainly prepare to come to class and be glad to read the exciting and relevant text we had chosen for the course. However, the students were not very well prepared for class, and more time had to be spent covering content than should have been necessary. In retrospect, it was not a good assumption that the students would read the text and be prepared for class. Quizzes over the reading would have increased the likelihood of the students coming more prepared for class.

Course Evaluations

Course evaluations were conducted by the Veteran Services Office and the Dean of Undergraduate Studies Office. The qualitative assessment results showed that student veterans who were new to the university benefitted more from the university experience portion of the course, which helped them to acclimate to the university, while the student veterans who were closer to graduation benefitted more from the career course component. Furthermore, the veterans reported that they needed more specific career assessments, such as the Self-Directed Search (Holland, 1994) and a personality assessment such as the Myers-Briggs Type Indicator (https://www.cpp.com/products/mbti/index.aspx), and to see how their individual profiles fit into the world of work. Students indicated that the time allotted for career exploration was too short.

Recommendations to improve the course in the future were to teach the career course for the full 16 weeks of the semester and target veterans who were in their senior years. Veterans who are freshmen, sophomores, or incoming transfer juniors would seem to benefit more by being in a university experience course customized with content specific to veterans.

Comparison to Other Career Courses Taught by the Instructor

This class was difficult to teach because we did not anticipate the age spread. Some of the veterans had completed one tour of active duty (3–4 years) and were still in their early 20s, and others had retired from over 30 years of service and had children of their own in college. The common identity was being a veteran. Some of the veterans in the class did have disabilities, but none of them turned in any accommodation requests from Disability Services.

Instructors' Weekly Reflections

The weekly meetings among instructors enabled us to better prepare for the next week of instruction by discussing the goals for each week. A few times we found we really needed to go back and review material previously presented because the students weren't clear on the expectations. For example, when we were teaching interviewing techniques and having the students conduct a mock interview, we found that some of the students only recorded 2 or 3 minutes of interview practice. We had to go back and clarify that they needed to record a minimum of 10 minutes for us to fairly evaluate their skill. We had assumed they would enjoy this tool and practice, and would not have to be given real specific guidelines, but that was not the case. There was also a great deal of confusion about the job search notebooks at the end of the class. In response, we made up some samples to show them what we were expecting and spent a little more time in small groups working on that assignment.

Student Feedback

While the feedback from students about the course was generally favorable, they did have some recommendations that have since been incorporated into the course. These include choice of instructor, addressing expectations, choice and sequencing of assignments, self-assessments, managing course discussions, and course structure.

Choice of Instructor

The importance of having an instructor who is a veteran seemed to be very important to these students. A picture is worth a thousand words, and seeing an instructor who has, in the eyes of the students, successfully accomplished what they are being encouraged to do becomes believable to them. If finding an instructor who is a veteran is difficult, a seasoned career instructor could deliver the course, but having regular guest speakers who are veterans would be strongly recommended.

Reviewing Expectations

In the beginning of the course, some time should be spent thoroughly explaining the expectations for the course. The fact that several hours will need to be spent outside of class to complete assignments, read, and prepare for the next class needs to be spelled out. Most military training takes place in the classroom, not outside of the classroom.

Assignments

Introduce practical assignments related to job searching early in the first couple of weeks of the course. Informational interviews could help validate the need to investigate thoroughly possible career interests. These interviews will also help students gain a more accurate picture of the qualifications and experience of professionals in these positions.

Self-Assessments

A complete battery of career assessments should be administered to identify career interests, personality profile, employment skills, and employment values. A significant amount of time should be spent in the first week or two of the course reviewing and interpreting the assessment results. In later weeks of the course, frequent review of assessments should be woven into the class discussions.

Summary

The veteran students in this class were a remarkable group and had each done extraordinary things in their service to the United States. They were also a challenging group because they did not accept much of the information that was presented in the class. They were skeptical and had some strong-held beliefs, such as how valuable their military experience would be to a civilian employer and that finding a job would be relatively easy. They were still very loyal and trusting of the military establishment, and had not yet become comfortable with trust outside of the military.

In one of the lectures, a typical timeline for a job search campaign using six months as the standard was covered. The tasks that would need to be performed month by month to move from initial selection of a job target to the first day on a new job were outlined. However, the class was not convinced that the timeline used was accurate. The fact that job search campaigns can typically take between three and six months is well documented (Hay, Rorrer, Rivera, Krannich, & Krannich, 2006), and up to eight hours a day during that period (Reardon, Lenz, Sampson, & Peterson, 2009). Students were judging the explanation based on their prior job-seeking experience for hourly positions.

These veteran students would have been very competitive and highly qualified job candidates for hourly positions. However, for salaried, professional, degreed positions, the competition would be more intense and the expectations significantly higher. Some months after the class was completed, and a number of these students had conducted professional level, degreed job-search campaigns, they returned and reported that they now believed the information that was taught to them in the class about the realities of the job search. Another hard learned recommendation we would suggest is beginning the course with more "military bearing" than "collegiate leniency." Veteran students in our course seemed to benefit, at least initially from more structure rather than less structure.

This course is still being offered. All of the feedback from this course was processed and the course was reshaped. Much of the content that was in the course related to job search skills is still in the course. A significant amount of information about the Veterans Administration and how veterans can access their benefits has been added to the course. There is still some content focused on transitioning into higher education and adapting to university life. The course is currently offered as a leadership course and taught by the Director of the Veterans Services Office.

References

Bloom, B. S. (1956). *Taxonomy of educational objectives, handbook I: The cognitive domain.* New York: David McKay Co.

Farley, J. I. (2010). *Military-to-civilian: Career transition guide* (2nd ed.). Indianapolis, IN: JIST Works.

Hay, M. T., Rorrer, L. H., Rivera, J. R., Krannich, R., & Krannich C. (2006). *Military transition to civilian success: The complete guide for veterans and their families.* Manassas Park, VA: Impact Publications.

Holland, J.L. (1994). *Occupations Finder,* Form R. Odessa, FL: Psychological Assessment Resources.

Osborn, D.S. (2008). *Teaching career development: A primer for instructors and presenters.* Broken Arrow, OK: National Career Development Association.

Osborn, D. S., Howard, D. K., & Leierer, S. (2007). The impact of a one credit six week career course on the dysfunctional career thoughts of diverse college freshmen. *The Career Development Quarterly, 55,* 365-377.

Reardon, R.C., Folsom, B., Lee, D. & Clark, J. (2011) *The effects of college career courses on learner outputs & outcomes: Technical report no. 53.* Tallahassee, FL: The Center for the Study of Technology in Counseling and Career Development.

Reardon, R.C., Lenz, J.G., Sampson, J.P., Jr. & Peterson, G.W. (2009). *Career development and planning: comprehensive approach* (3rd ed.). Mason, OH: Cengage Learning.

APPENDIX A

Glossary

Active Duty Military (AD): Individuals who have full time duty in the United States' active military, including those in the reserves who are on active duty or in training duty full time. This does not include those who are full time in the National Guard.

Air Reserve Technicians for the Reserves (ARTs): Federal civil service employees of their units for whom participating in the unit as a traditional Guardsman or Reservist is a condition of employment.

Armed Services Vocational Aptitude Battery (ASVAB): A multi-aptitude test used to identify civilian and military occupations that best match a person's aptitudes. This test is available free to high school students but must be scheduled (http://asvabprogram.com/asvabMobile/schedule.cfm).

DD Form 214: Provides a transcript of the person's service given upon leaving the military

DD Form 2648: See Pre-Separation Counseling Checklist

Disabled Veterans' Outreach Program Specialists (DVOPS): Vet Reps specific for veterans with disabilities

Enlisted Evaluation Report (EER): An evaluation form used by the United States Army for enlisted military

Enlisted Performance Report (EPR): An evaluation form used by the US Air Force.

Find Your Interests (FYI): An inventory that mimics the Self-Directed Search for the military. It is part of the ASVAB and generates a three letter Holland code.

Fitness Report (FITREP): An evaluation form used by the US Navy.

Forward Operating Base (FOB): Any secured area that is used to support military operations

Honorable Discharge: An honor bestowed on a service member due to receiving a good to excellent rating for service rendered

Individual Mobilization Augmentees (IMA)/Traditional: Individual "Weekend Warrior" job better known as "Citizen Soldiers," who work a regular civilian job, but train with their unit once a month. If activated and mobilized, they are required to drop everything and report to active duty.

Individual Transition Plan (ITP): A planning guide for separating military that includes a checklist and several planning worksheets.

Military and Family Life Consultants (MLFC):	Licensed clinical providers assist service members and their families with issues they may face through the cycle of deployment, from leaving their loved ones and possibly living and working in harm's way to reintegrating with their community and family
Military Occupational Specialties (MOS):	A military term representing the various enlisted occupational positions in the Army
Military Occupational Specialty Code (MOSC):	A nine character code used by the US Army and Marines that provides detailed information about the military member's MOS. Each character represents specific information, such as skill level, language identification, and so forth
Military OneSource:	Military OneSource uses a nationwide network of practitioners that provide short-term, solution-focused sessions that deal with veterans' adjustment issues, work life topics and emotional well-being issues
Military Sexual Trauma (MST):	Sexual trauma experienced within the military, including any sexual activity against the veteran where the individual was not a willing participant.
Montgomery GI Bill:	The MGI bill allows for up to 36 months of educational benefits. Enrollees pay $100 per month for 12 months and must complete a minimum service obligations.
National Guard:	A reserve force of the US Military with members represented from each states. The majority of National Guard hold a full time civilian job and serve for the Guard part time.
Officer Evaluation Report (OER):	An evaluation form used by the US Army for commissioned officers.
O*NET Military Crosswalk:	An occupational database that allows a comparison between military and civilian occupations.
Operations Enduring and Iraqi Freedom (OEF/OIF):	Refers to military conflicts in Afghanistan and Iraq.
Post 9/11 GI Bill:	Provides up to 36 months of financial support for education and housing for individuals with at least 90 days of aggregate service on or after 9/11/01 (including National Guard after 10/1/11), or individuals discharged with a service-connected disability after 30 days.
Pre-Separation Counseling Checklist:	A checklist created by the military to act as a record of services and benefits requested by the service member and/or provided to the service member. It may also serve to identify salient areas for inclusion on the Individual Transition Plan. Also see DD Form 2648.

Reserve Educational Assistance Program (REAP):	Contribution-based programs to provide service members with educational funding benefits.
Recently Separated Service members (RSS):	The term used to describe military service members that have been recently discharged or released from active military duty.
Separation:	Refers to the process of separating from active duty, whether due to retirement or discharge.
Servicemembers Opportunity College (SOC) Consortium:	Consists of about 1,800 colleges that allow military members to transfer credits and count military experience for credit across the schools in the consortium.
Traumatic Brain Injury:	A severe injury to the brain that is caused by an external force.
Transition Assistance Program (TAP):	A program created as a result of a law that formed a partnership among the Departments of Defense, Veterans Affairs, Transportation, and the Veteran's Employment and Training Service, a division of the Department of Labor. TAP provides workshops on all aspects of career decision making and job search, as well as information on benefits available to veterans.
TRICARE:	The health care program for military service members, retirees and their families.
Veterans Educational Assistance Program (VEAP):	Contribution-based programs to provide service members with educational funding benefits, for those Entered service for the first time between January 1, 1977, and June 30, 1985.
Veterans:	Individuals who have "served in the active duty military, Coast Guard, uniformed Public Health Service, and the uniformed National Oceanic and Atmospheric Administration, reservists called to active duty, and those disabled while on active duty training" (US Department of Veterans Affairs, VA, 2010, p. 51).
Vet Reps:	"Vet Reps" or veterans employment representatives are employment specialists which provide funding exclusively for servicing veterans, transitioning service members, and their spouses.
VetSuccess:	The website for Veterans Affairs, (www.vetsuccess.gov), aimed at providing resources for transitioning veterans.
Veterans Upward Bound (VUB):	Offers academic preparation, refresher courses, tutoring, mentoring, assistance with applications for admission, financial aid, GI bill, and scholarships.

Appendix B: Pre-Separation Checklist

PRESEPARATION COUNSELING CHECKLIST
FOR ACTIVE COMPONENT (AC), ACTIVE GUARD RESERVE (AGR), ACTIVE RESERVE (AR), FULL TIME SUPPORT (FTS), AND RESERVE PROGRAM ADMINISTRATOR (RPA) SERVICE MEMBERS
(Please read Privacy Act Statement and Instructions in Section III before completing this form.)

SECTION I - PRIVACY ACT STATEMENT

AUTHORITY: 10 U.S.C. 1142, Preparation Counseling; E.O. 9397, as amended (SSN).

PRINCIPAL PURPOSE(S): To record preparation services and benefits requested by and provided to Service members; to identify preparation counseling areas of interest as a basis for development of an Individual Transition Plan (ITP). The signed preparation counseling checklist will be maintained in the Service member's official personnel file. Title 10, USC 1142, requires that not later than 90 days before the date of separation, for anticipated losses, preparation counseling for Service members be made available. For unanticipated losses, preparation counseling shall be made available as soon as possible.

ROUTINE USE(S): None.

DISCLOSURE: Disclosure of SSN is mandatory. Disclosure of other information in Section II is voluntary; however, it may not be possible to initiate preparation counseling and other transition assistance services or develop an Individual Transition Plan (ITP) for a Service member if the information is not provided.

SECTION II - PERSONAL INFORMATION *(To be filled out by all applicants)*

1. NAME a. Last Name / b. First Name / c. Middle Initial	2. SSN	3. GRADE	4. DATE OF BIRTH (YYYYMMDD)

5. SERVICE (X one)	5.a. COMPONENT	6. DUTY STATION	7. ANTICIPATED DATE OF SEPARATION (YYYYMMDD)
ARMY	AC	a. MILITARY INSTALLATION/CITY	
MARINE CORPS	AGR		
NAVY	AR	b. STATE c. ZIP CODE	7.a. I AM (X one): Retiring / Separating Voluntarily / Separating Involuntarily
AIR FORCE	RPA		
COAST GUARD	FTS		

8. DATE CHECKLIST PREPARED (YYYYMMDD)	8.a. Place an X in this box ONLY if you have 89 days or less remaining on active duty before separation or retirement *(Please read the following instructions: If separating or retiring and you have 89 days or less remaining on active duty before your separation or retirement, why was your preparation counseling not conducted earlier? Please go to Section VI - REMARKS and check the response that best describes why preparation counseling was not conducted earlier.)*

9. Is your spouse/family member/legal guardian/designee present during preparation counseling? (X one)　☐ YES　☐ NO　☐ N/A

9.a. Are you willing to be contacted after separation or retirement regarding the value of the transition assistance programs and services you received? (X one)　☐ YES　☐ NO

SECTION III - INSTRUCTIONS

All transitioning Service members shall read these instructions before completing Sections IV, V, and VI of this form. After being counseled, Service member shall sign and date the form in items 28.a. and 28.b.

This form will be used for Active Component (AC), Active Guard Reserve (AGR), Active Reserve (AR), Full Time Support (FTS), and Reserve Program Administrator (RPA) Service members.

(1) Items checked "YES" indicate that you require additional information or referral to a subject matter expert on the installation or to an appropriate person in another agency or organization outside of DoD or attendance at a scheduled employment or VA session (Section IV).

(2) Shaded areas on the form mean: (a) the information is not applicable (example: item 11.b. is shaded under "Spouse" because DD Form 2586, "Verification of Military Experience and Education - VMET", does not apply to spouses); or (b) the item is referring to a Web site address and URLs require no further explanation. URLs are provided so Service members can research information at their leisure on a given topic or subject.

(3) **Department of Labor TAP Employment Workshop:** In accordance with DoDI 1332.35, AC, AGR, AR, FTS, and RPA separating and retiring Service members who check "YES" in item 11.a. on DD Form 2648, "Preparation Counseling Checklist", shall be released to complete the Department of Labor (DOL) Transition Assistance Program (TAP) Employment Workshop in its entirety. Service members will be exempt from normal duty the full 24 hour period of each DOL workshop day and the 12 hours immediately preceding and following the DOL workshop. In the event that a DOL Workshop is unavailable, the Service member will attend a military equivalent employment workshop conducted by the Military Services.

(4) **Veterans Benefits Briefing:** In accordance with DoDI 1332.35, all separating and retiring Service members who check "YES" in item 19 shall be released to complete the Veterans Benefits Briefing sponsored and offered by the Department of Veterans Affairs (VA) in its entirety. Service members will be exempt from normal duty the full 24 hour period of each VA Benefits Briefing day and the 12 hours immediately preceding and following the VA Benefits Briefing.

(5) **Disabled Transition Assistance Program (DTAP):** In accordance with DoDI 1332.35, all separating and retiring Service members who check "YES" in item 20 (with special emphasis on Wounded, Ill, or Injured) who have or think they have a service-connected disability, are awaiting a medical discharge, or have incurred an injury or illness while on active duty, or aggravated a pre-existing condition, and those referred to a Physical Evaluation Board or placed in a medical hold status by their Service, shall be released to complete the DTAP briefing sponsored by VA. Spouses/Family Member/Legal Guardian/Designee are encouraged to attend the DTAP briefing. Service members will be exempt from normal duty the full 24 hour period of each VA DTAP Briefing day and the 12 hours immediately preceding and following the VA DTAP Briefing.

PRESEPARATION COUNSELING CHECKLIST FOR AC, AGR, AR, FTS, AND RPA SERVICE MEMBERS	NAME *(Last, First, Middle Initial)*					SSN	

SECTION IV

Please indicate *(by checking either YES or NO)* whether you (or if accompanied by your spouse/family member/legal guardian/designee if applicable) desire additional counseling for the following benefits and services to which you may be entitled. All benefits and services checked YES should be used to develop your Individual Transition Plan (ITP). The following benefits and services available to all Service members, unless otherwise specified, will be explained by the Transition/Command Career Counselor.

	SERVICE MEMBER		SPOUSE		REFERRED TO
	YES	NO	YES	NO	
10. EFFECTS OF A CAREER CHANGE					
11. EMPLOYMENT ASSISTANCE					
a. Do you want to attend the Department of Labor sponsored Transition Assistance Employment Workshops or Service sponsored Transition workshops/seminars?					
b. Verification of Military Experience and Training (VMET) (DD Form 2586). Do you want a copy of your VMET document? If yes, go to www.dmdc.osd.mil/vmet to print your VMET document and cover letter.					
c. Counselor will provide information on civilian occupations corresponding to Military occupations (see Occupational Information Network (O*NET website) at www.online.onetcenter.org/crosswalk and related assistance programs) and civilian occupations related to assistance programs.					
(1) Licensing, Certifications and Apprenticeship Information					
(a) Department of Labor www.careeronestop.org/CREDENTIALING/CredentialingHome.asp					
(b) U.S. Army Credentialing On-line https://www.cool.army.mil					
(c) U.S. Military Apprenticeship Program https://usmap.cnet.navy.mil/usmapss					
(d) DANTES www.dantes.doded.mil/dantes_web/danteshome.asp					
(e) Navy Cool Website https://www.cool.navy.mil					
d. TurboTAP.org (www.TurboTAP.org) and other programs, tools, and resources					
(1) Employment Hub www.turboTAP.org/portal/transition/resources/Employment_Hub					
(2) Hire Vets First www.hirevetsfirst.dol.gov/					
(3) State Job Boards www.careeronestop.org/jobsearch/cos_jobsites.aspx					
(4) DOL REALifelines www.hirevetsfirst.dol.gov/realifelines/index.asp					
e. Public and Community Service Opportunities www.turboTAP.org/portal/transition/lifestyles/Employment/Public_and_Community_Service_PACS_Registry_Program					
f. Teacher and Teacher's Aide Opportunities/Troops to Teachers www.proudtoserveagain.com					
g. Federal Employment Opportunities					
(1) www.usajobs.opm.gov					
(2) www.go-defense.com					
(3) Information on Veterans Preference in Federal Employment					
(4) Information on Veterans Federal Procurement Opportunities					
(5) Office of Personnel Management (OPM) Special Hiring Authorities					
h. Hiring Preference in Non-Appropriated Fund (NAF) jobs (Eligible Involuntary Separatees)					
i. State Employment Agencies					
(1) Career One Stop Centers www.careeronestop.org/jobsearch/cos_jobsites.aspx					
(2) Workforce Investment Act (WIA)					
j. Information concerning veterans small business ownership and entrepreneurship programs					
(1) Small Business Administration www.sba.gov/aboutsba/sbaprograms/ovbd/ and www.score.org SBA Patriot Express Loan					
(2) National Veteran's Business Development Corporation www.veteranscorp.org					
k. Information on employment and reemployment rights and obligations (USERRA) for Active Duty Service Members *(Chapter 43, Title 38 U.S. Code)*					
l. Information on "Priority of Service" for veterans in receipt of employment, training, and placement services provided under qualified job training programs of the Department of Labor					

PRESEPARATION COUNSELING CHECKLIST FOR AC, AGR, AR, FTS, AND RPA SERVICE MEMBERS	NAME *(Last, First, Middle Initial)*		SSN		

SECTION IV *(Continued)*	SERVICE MEMBER		SPOUSE		REFERRED TO
	YES	NO	YES	NO	
12. RELOCATION ASSISTANCE *NOTE: Status of Forces Agreement limitations apply to overseas Service members.*					
a. Permissive (TDY/TAD) and Excess leave					
*b. Travel and Transportation Allowances (see Note above)					
13. CONTACT INFORMATION FOR HOUSING COUNSELING ASSISTANCE portal.hud.gov/portal/page/portal/HUD					
14. EDUCATION/TRAINING					
a. Education benefits (Post 9-11 GI Bill Chapter 33), (Montgomery GI Bill Chapter 30), (Veterans Educational Assistance Program), (Vietnam-era, etc.) www.gibill.va.gov					
b. U.S. Department of Education Federal Aid Programs www.FederalStudentAid.ed.gov					
c. Other Federal, State, or local education/training programs and options					
15. PHYSICAL AND MENTAL HEALTH WELL-BEING					
a. Information on availability of Healthcare and Mental Health Services (Post-traumatic stress disorder, anxiety disorders, depression, suicidal ideations, combat operational/stress, or other mental health conditions associated with service in the Armed Forces)					
(1) Transitional Healthcare Benefit/TRICARE (for eligibility and additional information go to: www.tricare.mil or www.tricare.mil/Factsheets/browsetopic.cfm) (click on Transitional Assistance Management Program)					
(2) VA Health Administration www1.va.gov/health/index.asp					
(3) VA Vet Center www.vetcenter.va.gov					
(4) State and local healthcare and mental health services					
b. Describe healthcare and other benefits to which the member may be entitled under the laws administered by the Secretary of Veterans Affairs - www.va.gov					
(1) VA health care					
(2) VA dental care					
16. HEALTH AND LIFE INSURANCE					
a. Continued Health Care Benefits Program - Option to purchase 18-month conversion health insurance. Concurrent pre-existing condition coverage with purchase of conversion health insurance www.tricare.mil/mybenefit/home/overview/SpecialPrograms/CHCBP					
b. Veterans Group Life Insurance (VGLI) www.insurance.va.gov/sglisite/vgli.htm and www.turboTAP.org websites					
c. Servicemembers' Group Life Insurance (SGLI) www.insurance.va.gov/sglisite/default.htm and www.turboTAP.org websites					
d. Traumatic Injury Protection Program (TSGLI) www.insurance.va.gov/sglisite/tsgli/expandedbenefits.htm and www.turboTAP.org websites					
e. Family Servicemembers' Group Life Insurance (FSGLI) www.insurance.va.gov/sglisite/fsgli/sglifam.htm and www.turboTAP.org websites					
f. Service-Disabled Veterans Insurance (S-DVI) www.insurance.va.gov/inForceGliSite/buying/SDVI.htm and www.turboTAP.org websites					
g. Veterans' Mortgage Life Insurance (VMLI) www.insurance.va.gov/inForceGliSite/buying/VMLI.htm and www.turboTAP.org websites					
h. For more information on Veterans Life Insurance, visit: www.insurance.va.gov					
i. Transitional Health and Dental Care Benefit - for eligibility criteria and additional information, go to: www.tricare.mil and www.tricare.mil/dental/TRDP_Eligibility.cfm					
17. FINANCES					
a. Financial Management (TSP, Retirement, SBP, military vs. civilian pay and benefits)					
b. Separation pay (Eligible Involuntary Separatees)					
c. Unemployment Compensation					
d. General money management (budgeting, debt reduction)					
e. Personal savings and investing					

PRESEPARATION COUNSELING CHECKLIST FOR AC, AGR, AR, FTS, AND RPA SERVICE MEMBERS	NAME (Last, First, Middle Initial)														SSN			

SECTION IV (Continued)	SERVICE MEMBER		SPOUSE		REFERRED TO
	YES	NO	YES	NO	
18. RESERVE AFFILIATION					
19. Do you want to attend the Veterans Benefits Briefing? (See section III, Instructions, item 4.)					
20. DISABLED VETERANS BENEFITS					
a. Do you want to attend the Disabled Transition Assistance Program (DTAP) Briefing? See Section III - Instructions, item 5 and VA Vocational Rehabilitation and Employment Service at www.vba.va.gov/bln/vre					
b. VA Disability Benefits www.vba.va.gov/VBA/benefits/factsheets					
c. Benefits Delivery at Discharge and Quick Start www.vba.va.gov/predischarge					
21. STATE VETERANS BENEFITS					
22. 2-YEAR COMMISSARY AND EXCHANGE PRIVILEGES (Eligible Involuntary Separatees)					
23. LEGAL ASSISTANCE					

24. POST GOVERNMENT (MILITARY) SERVICE EMPLOYMENT RESTRICTION COUNSELING
Information on post government (military) employment counseling (restrictions on employment, imposed by statute and regulation) shall be conducted by Services as appropriate. Transition/Command Career Counselors shall refer separating and retiring Service members to an installation legal office (Staff Judge Advocate or Counselor's Office) to ensure they receive a post government (military) employment restrictions briefing or counseling from an ethics official.

25. INDIVIDUAL TRANSITION PLAN (ITP)

a. As a separating Service member, after receiving Preseparation Counseling information and completing this checklist, you and your spouse/ family member/legal guardian/designee (if applicable) are entitled to receive assistance in developing an Individual Transition Plan (ITP) based on the areas of interest you have identified on this checklist. The Preseparation Counseling Checklist addresses a variety of transition services and benefits to which you may be entitled. Each individual is strongly encouraged to take advantage of the opportunity to develop an ITP. The purpose of the ITP is to identify educational, training, and employment objectives and to develop a plan to help you achieve these objectives. It is the Military Department's responsibility to offer Service members the opportunity and assistance they need to develop an ITP. It is the Service member's responsibility to develop an ITP based on his/her specific objectives and the objectives of his or her spouse, if appropriate.

	SERVICE MEMBER		SPOUSE	
Based upon information received during Preseparation Counseling, do you and/or your spouse/family member/ legal guardian/designee desire assistance in developing your ITP? If YES, the Transition staff/counselor/ Command Career Counselor is available to assist you (see www.TurboTap.org website).	YES	NO	YES	NO

b. To assist your transition counselor, choose the answer that best describes your post-military goal(s) (X all that apply)

☐ I already have post-military employment. ☐ I plan to go to school and use my VA education benefits.

☐ I plan to get a job and start work as soon as possible. ☐ I don't know what I plan to do.

☐ Other (please describe/write in)

SECTION V - LANGUAGE SKILLS/REGIONAL EXPERTISE

Counselors will ensure all transitioning Service members, Active, Guard and Reserve with language skills and/or regional expertise complete Item 26.

26. The Department of Defense and other Federal agencies have placed a high level of importance on critical foreign language skills and regional expertise to meet emerging requirements during times of need, crisis, and/or national emergency. The Department of Defense and other Federal agencies may want to contact you in the future to determine if you would be willing to volunteer your services or to offer you potential employment that would take advantage of your language proficiency and/or regional expertise.

a. Do you consent to being contacted by the Department of Defense for such purposes?	YES	NO
b. Do you consent to having the Department of Defense share your information with other Federal agencies for such purposes?	YES	NO

PRESEPARATION COUNSELING CHECKLIST FOR AC, AGR, AR, FTS, AND RPA SERVICE MEMBERS	NAME *(Last, First, Middle Initial)*	SSN

SECTION VI - REMARKS *(Attach additional pages if necessary)*

Complete the following ONLY if you placed an X in Item 8.a. *(See page 1, Section II, item 8.a.)*

27. MY COUNSELING WAS CONDUCTED 89 DAYS OR LESS BEFORE MY SEPARATION OR RETIREMENT BECAUSE OF: *(X one)*

☐ Mission requirements ☐ Legal separation

☐ Personal reasons ☐ Change in career decision

☐ Medical separation/discharge ☐ Other *(Please provide a brief explanation)*

28. SERVICE MEMBER ACKNOWLEDGEMENT

By signing and dating this form, you, the Service member, are acknowledging that you received Preseparation Counseling on the date below (item 28.b.), and that you understand the transition benefits and services available to assist you in your transition as required by Title 10, U.S.C., Chapter 58, Section 1142.

a. SERVICE MEMBER SIGNATURE	b. DATE *(YYYYMMDD)*	c. TRANSITION COUNSELOR SIGNATURE	d. DATE *(YYYYMMDD)*

APPENDIX C

Military-Related Websites

Branch Sites

Air Force Personnel Center
  afcommunity.af.mil/transition

Army Career and Alumni Program (ACAP)
  acap.army.mil

Coast Guard
  uscg.mil/worklife/transition_assistance.asp

Marines
  usmc-mccs.org/tamp/index.cfm

Navy
  .cnic.navy.mi

Crisis Support

Veterans Crisis Line
  veteranscrisisline.net

Education

Defense Activity for Non-Traditional Education Support (DANTES)
  dantes.doded.mil/DANTES_Homepage.html

GI Bill
  gibill.va.gov

VA Education Benefits and Services
  gibill.va.gov

Veterans Upward Bound
  navub.org

Government Support Sites

Career OneStop
  careeronestop.org/jobsearch/cos_jobsites.aspx

Faith-Based and Neighborhood Partnerships
  va.gov/cfbnpartnerships

Military OneSource
  militaryonesource.com

National Association of State Directors of Veterans Affairs (NASDVA)
  nasdva.net

National Resource Directory
  .nationalresourcedirectory.org

Office of Veterans Business Development
  sba.gov/about-offices-content/1/2985

Returning Service Members (OEF/OIF)
  oefoif.va.gov

US Department of Veterans Affairs
  va.gov

US Office of Personnel Management Vet Guide
  opm.gov/staffingPortal/Vetguide.asp

Veterans Benefits Administration
  vba.va.gov

Veterans' Employment and Training Service
  dol.gov/vets/aboutvets/main.htm

Vet Success
  vetsuccess.gov

Healthcare

Disability Compensation
  vabenefits.vba.va.gov

DoD Mental Health
  militarymentalhealth.org

Transitional Healthcare Benefit/TRICARE
  tricare.mil

VA Disability Benefits
  vba.va.gov/VBA/benefits/factsheets

VA Health Administration
  va.gov/health/index.asp

VA Health Care Eligibility
  va.gov/healtheligibility

VA Mental Health
  mentalhealth.va.gov

VA Vet Center
  vetcenter.va.gov

Housing

Homeless Veterans Program
  va.gov/homeless/index.asp

National Association of State Veterans Homes
  nasvh.org

National Coalition for Homeless Veterans
  nchv.org

US Department of Housing & Urban Development

    portal.hud.gov/portal/page/portal/HUD

VA Home Loan Guaranty
    homeloans.va.gov

Veteran Justice Outreach Initiative
    va.gov/HOMELESS/VJO.asp

Job Search Sites

America's Heroes at Work
    americasheroesatwork.gov

Build Your Career
    va.gov/jobs

Career Transition Adviser
    dol.gov/elaws/vets/realifelines/menu.htm

Civilian Jobs
    civilianjobs.com

Civilian Job News
    civilianjobnews.com

Corporate Gray
    corporategray.com

Feds Hire Vets
    fedshirevets.gov

G.I. Jobs
    gijobs.com

Jobs for Vets
    jobsforvetsalpha.org/id2.html

Military Connection
    militaryconnection.com

Military Hire
    militaryhire.com

Military to Federal Jobs Crosswalk
    mil2fedjobs.com/index.htm

My Next Move
    mynextmove.org/vets

National Resource Directory
    nationalresourcedirectory.gov

REALifelines: Veterans' Employment and Recruit Military
    recruitmilitary.com

Riley Guide
    rileyguide.com/vets.html

Troops to Teachers
    proudtoserveagain.com

Veterans Employment Center
    military.com/Careers/Home

Licensing, Certifications and Apprenticeship Information

Database of Accredited Postsecondary Institutions and Programs
    ope.ed.gov/accreditation

Servicemembers Opportunity College (SOC) Consortium
    dantes.doded.mil/Sub%20Pages/Higher_Ed/HigherEd_SOC.html

US Army Credentialing Opportunities Online
    cool.army.mil

US Department of Education's page on regional and national institutional accrediting agencies
    ed.gov/admins/finaid/accred/accreditation_pg6.html

US Military Apprenticeship Program
    usmap.cnet.navy.mil/usmapss

US Navy Credentialing Opportunities Online
    cool.navy.mil

Workforce Credentials Information Center
    careeronestop.org/CREDENTIALING/CredentialingHome.asp

Minority Veterans

Center for Minority Veterans
    va.gov/centerforminorityveterans

Native American Veterans Association (NNAVA)
    nativeamericanveteransassoc.org

Tuskegee Airmen
    tuskegeeairmen.org

Military-to-Civilian Transitions

Career One Stop
    careeronestop.org/MilitaryTransition

Turbo Tap
turbotap.org/

Occupational Crosswalks

Mil2FedJobs Federal Jobs Crosswalk
Mil2FedJobs.com

O*NET
onetonline.org/crosswalk/MOC

Personal Records

Military Records Correction (SF Form293)
archives.gov/veterans/military-servicerecords/
correcting-records.html

Transcripts of education and training credits from branch of service
turbotap.org/portal/Tap_toolkit_2011/Career_
Toolkit/module8/player.html

Veterans Service Records
archives.gov/veterans/military-service-records

Self-Employment

Center for Veterans Enterprise &Business
vetbiz.gov

Veteranscorp
veteranscorp.org

US Small Business Administration for Veterans
sba.gov/vets

Self-Knowledge

ASVAB Career Exploration Program
asvabprogram.com

Military Skills Translator
military.com/skills-translator/mos-translator

VA Military Skills Translators
vetsuccess.gov/military_skills_translators

Spouse and Family Support Sites

After Deployment
afterdeployment.org

Career One Stop Military Support Resources
careeronestop.org/militaryspouse

DoD Family Benefits
defenselink.mil/ra/documents/benefitsguide.pdf

Military and Family Life Consultants
www.mhngs.com

Office of Survivors Assistance
va.gov/survivors/

Unmet Needs Program
unmetneeds.org

VA Caregiver Support
caregiver.va.gov

VA Kids
va.gov/kids

Statistics

Bureau of Labor Statistics, Vets
bls.gov/news.release/vet.toc.htm

Census Data on Veterans
census.gov/hhes/veterans

VA Health Services Research & Development
hsrd.research.va.gov

VA Statistics
va.gov/vetdata

Vet Rep

Veterans Employment Representative
taonline.com/VetReps/SearchVetRep.asp.

Veteran Service Organizations

American Ex-prisoners of War
axpow.org

American Legion
legion.org

American Veterans
amvets.org

Armed Forces Foundation
armedforcesfoundation.org

Disabled American Veterans
dav.org

Employer Support of the Guard and Reserve
esgr.org

MOPH-Military Order of Purple Heart
purpleheart.org

Paralyzed Veterans of America
pva.org

US Chamber of Commerce
uschamber.com/veterans/events

Veterans of Foreign Wars
vfw.org

War-Specific Veterans' Sites

BosniaLINK
dtic.mil/bosnia/index.html

Gulf War Veterans
www.gulfwarvets.com

Vietnam Veterans of America
www.vva.org

WWII U.S. Veterans
ww2.vet.org

Korean War Veterans Association:
www.kwva.org

Women Veterans

Center for Women Veterans
va.gov/womenvet

Defense Advisory Committee on Women in the Services (DACOWITS)
dacowits.defense.gov

Military Woman
militarywoman.org

National Association of State Women Veteran Coordinators
naswvc.com

Women's Overseas Service League
wosl.org

Women Veterans Health Program
womenshealth.va.gov

APPENDIX D

Veteran Success Syllabus

Fall

Monday/Wednesday **3:05 – 4:20 PM**

Instructor: **Title:**
E-mail: **Office Location:**
Phone: **Office Hours:**

Course Description

This three-credit, discussion-based and experiential, elective course is designed to facilitate a successful transition to university expectations and campus life as well as develop knowledge and skills for entering civilian employment. Overall concepts investigated include exploring campus resources, identity development, personal accountability, civic engagement, academic skills, career exploration and job search skills. The course seeks to assist military veteran students toward self-actualization and integration into the life of the campus community and prepare for the transition from academic life to civilian employment.

Course Goals and Objectives

This course is designed as an introductory seminar in which students will have the opportunity to explore the overall building blocks for success in college and in life, understanding that the journey of college is a time of personal growth and change and begins with the identification and clarification of values, establishing a sense of identity, and exploring the values and thoughts of others. In addition, understanding their individual interests, values and skills students will be able to identify their occupational choices for fitting into the civilian world of work. They will also be prepared to make informed career decisions and acquire the skills to conduct an effective job search campaign. This course will emphasize the following objectives:

1. Understanding the process of self-direction through establishing goals, using effective problem solving and critical thinking skills, and identifying the appropriate resources to succeed in reaching those goals
   a. Become familiar with a wide range of campus resources
   b. Develop short- and long-term goals
   c. Demonstrate effective problem-solving and critical thinking skills
   d. Make an informed choice of a career goal and write a career objective
   e. Exercise decision-making skills in selecting employers of interest
2. Exploring and developing the academic and personal skills necessary to succeed in college and as a self-directed, lifelong learner
   a. Understand individual learning preferences and the impact on the selection of learning strategies
   b. Identify the academic strategies most appropriate for them
   c. Identify and utilize appropriate educational resources as needed
3. Developing a respect for the role and responsibility that each individual plays as a connected and engaged citizen of diverse communities
   a. Work effectively within a group setting
   b. Articulate the importance of becoming engaged USF students
4. Relating knowledge of self, values, and goals to the exploration of careers, interests, and intended majors'
   a. Identify and understand personal values as they relate to career choice
   b. Identify the basic knowledge, skills, and professional requirements associated with the principles of a selected career field
   c. Identify the links between selected courses and potential careers thereby solidifying their choice of an academic major
5. Develop effective job search skills and a plan for transitioning from academic life to civilian employment
   a. Create an effective professional resume
   b. Demonstrate competitive interview skills
   c. Prepare and deliver an elevator speech
   d. Conduct informational interviews with professionals working in their occupation of interest

6. Engaging in self-reflection throughout the semester on personal development and its interaction with educational and career goals
    a. Develop and practice the skill of self-reflection
    b. Articulate how the General Education Curriculum connects to personal development and educational goals
    c. Develop an individual educational plan
    d. Demonstrate the skills necessary to select, schedule, and register for courses
    e. Compile a job search notebook which will administratively organize professional level job search campaign
    f. Develop and document an individual career plan

Required Texts

- Conway, J., & Rathburn, M. (Eds.). (2010). *Experience USF* (8th ed.). Boston, MA: Pearson.
- Hay, M.T., Rivera, J.R., Krannich, R.L.& Krannich C.R. (2006). *Military transition to civilian success.* Manassas Park, VA: Impact Publications.
- Liptak, J.J. (2009). *Job Search Knowldege Scale (JSKS).* Indianapolis, IN. JIST Publishing. **(purchase 2 copies for Pre and Post evaluation)**
- One 3 Ring Notebook Binder 1 ½ to 2 " and a set of dividers

---

Course Policies

Attendance/Participation: In order for this class to function properly, attendance and <u>active</u> participation is expected from all students. Showing up to class but not contributing to discussions or activities may result in a loss of participation points. Likewise, arriving late or leaving early may cost you participation points for that day.

Each absence from class will result in a <u>1 point</u> deduction from your participation grade. Extenuating circumstances such as a family emergency, extended illness, or observance of a religious holiday will be considered on a case-by-case basis. You are expected to e-mail your instructor in advance if you expect to miss class. You are also responsible for determining what was covered in class and for completing any assignments that are due.

Late Assignments: You are expected to turn in all assignments on the due date noted in the Class Agenda (page 4). For each class meeting that an assignment is late, your grade for that assignment will be reduced by <u>10 percent</u>.

Classroom Behavior: You are expected to arrive to class <u>on time</u> and prepared to participate in all class activities, as well as turn in any assignments that are due that day. In return, you have the right to expect that your instructor will come to class ready to teach. E-mails will be answered and graded assignments will be returned in a timely manner.

One purpose of this class is to create a safe environment where everyone is encouraged to share their opinions, emotions, and aspirations in class discussions. Please respect your classmates by maintaining confidentiality and not discussing this information outside of the classroom. Any student exhibiting rude or disrespectful behavior will be asked to leave class and will lose participation points for that day.

Cell phones and other electronic devices (including laptop computers) are <u>NOT</u> permitted in class. Please turn them off before entering the classroom and do not leave class to answer a phone call. *Exception: During the Career Development portion of the class laptops will be used during some class meetings for group work to be done in class.*

<u>Participation points will be deducted at the instructor's discretion for any inappropriate behavior</u>. This includes, but is not limited to: disrespectful behavior toward your instructor and/or classmates, arriving late to class or leaving early, texting, playing games, doing work for another class, excessive talking, or other disruption (such as a ringing cell phone). For more information concerning appropriate student behavior, please refer to the Student Code of Conduct at http://www.sa.usf.edu/handbook/USF_Student_Handbook.pdf.

Student/Instructor Communication: Your USF e-mail address is considered the official means of communication among students and instructor. Personal e-mail accounts, such as AOL or Hotmail, should not be used. In addition, this course will involve frequent use of Blackboard. You are expected to log in to your Blackboard and USF e-mail accounts at least twice each week to check for new announcements and assignments. If you do not have Internet access at home, you may utilize the library or computer labs on campus. You will be held responsible for any assignments or announcements that are posted on Blackboard or sent to your student e-mail account. All e-mails to your instructor will be answered in a timely fashion.

Emergency Closure: In the event of an emergency, it may be necessary for USF to suspend normal operations. During this time, USF may opt to continue delivery of instruction through methods that include but are not limited to: Blackboard, Elluminate, Skype, and email messaging and/or an alternate schedule. It's the responsibility of the student to monitor Blackboard site for each class for course specific communication, and the main USF, College, and department websites, emails, and MoBull messages for important general information.

Accommodations for Students with Disabilities: Students with disabilities are responsible for registering with Students with Disabilities Services in order to receive academic accommodations. SDS encourages students to notify instructors of accommodation needs at least 5 business days prior to needing the accommodation. A letter from SDS must accompany this request. See Student Responsibilities at http://www.asasd.usf.edu/Students.htm and Faculty Responsibilities at http://www.asasd.usf.edu/faculty.htm.

USF Policy on Religious Observances: All students have a right to expect that the University will reasonably accommodate their religious observances, practices, and beliefs. Please notify your instructor in writing before the second class meeting if you intend to be absent from a class, in accordance with this policy.

Academic Honesty: You are expected to be familiar with the Academic Dishonesty and Disruption of Academic Process Policy found in the USF 2010-2011 Undergraduate Catalog. Neither cheating nor plagiarism (defined as unattributed quotation of the exact words of a published text or another's writing, or the unattributed borrowing of original ideas by paraphrase from a published text) will be tolerated.

The University of South Florida has an account with an automated plagiarism detection service which allows instructors to submit student assignments to be checked for plagiarism. Your instructor reserves the right to submit assignments to this detection system. Assignments are compared automatically with a database of journal articles, web articles, and previously submitted papers. The instructor receives a report showing exactly how a student's paper was plagiarized.

Dropping/Withdrawing from Class: The last day to drop this class (to receive a refund) is August 27. The last day to withdraw (with a grade of "W" - no academic penalty) is October 30. You are strongly advised to consult with your academic advisor and the Office of Financial Aid (if applicable) before dropping or withdrawing from any class.

Incomplete Grades: An incomplete (I) grade is temporarily given in rare instances when a student is passing, but due to unforeseeable circumstances he/she is unable to complete the course requirements before the end of the term. Please refer to the "I" Grade Policy found in the USF 2010-2011 Undergraduate Catalog for more information.

Assignments and Grading

Grades are issued based on the total points earned for class attendance, participation, and completion of the assigned readings, self-assessments, papers, and activities. Grades will not be negotiated or curved. This means you should invest time in preparing for class and submitting your best effort on all assigned work. Since this is a college-level course, you are expected to write in a scholarly manner using proper grammar, punctuation, and sentence structure. Research sources are to be properly cited using MLA or APA format. All assignments must be typed unless otherwise indicated, and some must be submitted electronically through Blackboard's Safe Assignment. Specific instructions for each assignment will be posted on Blackboard.

Below are the grading distributions (including the plus/minus system) that will be used for this course:

Assignment	Point Value
Journal: My Expectations of This Course	2
Campus Resource Group Assignment	5
Journal: Juggling Multiple Roles	2
Discussion Board: Strategies for Success	2
Article Response	3
Academic Biography	10
Journal: My Budget	2
Pamphlet: Writing an Objective Statement	3
Final Resume	8
Final Cover Letter	4
Five Employer Research Exercises	5
Elevator Speech	6
Recorded Optimal Interview	8
Job Search Notebook	10
Two Informational Interviews	8
Course Reflection Essay	7
Attendance/Participation	15
Total	**100**

Overall Percentage	Letter Grade
97 - 100%	A+
94 - 96%	A
90 - 93%	A-
87 - 89%	B+
84 - 86%	B
80 - 83%	B-
77 - 79%	C+
74 - 76%	C
70 - 73%	C-
67 - 69%	D+
64 - 66%	D
60 - 63%	D-
59 or below	F

Index